The Power of a
PRAYING®
Couple

STORMIE
OMARTIAN

HARVEST HOUSE PUBLISHERS
EUGENE, OREGON

Cover design by Bryce Williamson

Cover images © by antishock, antart, Komar art / Shutterstock

Back cover author photo © Michael Gomez Photography

Interior design by Chad Dougherty

For bulk, special sales, or ministry purchases, please call 1-800-547-8979.
Email: CustomerService@hhpbooks.com

This logo is a federally registered trademark of The Hawkins Children's LLC. Harvest House Publishers, Inc., is the exclusive licensee of the trademark.

THE POWER OF A PRAYING is a registered trademark of The Hawkins Children's LLC. Harvest House Publishers, Inc., is the exclusive licensee of the federally registered trademark THE POWER OF A PRAYING.

Italics in Scripture verses are emphasis from the author.

The Power of a Praying® Couple
Copyright © 2024 by Stormie Omartian
Published by Harvest House Publishers
Eugene, Oregon 97408
www.harvesthousepublishers.com

ISBN 978-0-7369-8264-1 (pbk)
ISBN 978-0-7369-8265-8 (eBook)

Library of Congress Control Number: 2024935688

Printed in the United States of America

24 25 26 27 28 29 30 31 32 / BP / 10 9 8 7 6 5 4 3 2 1

If there is any consolation in Christ,
if any comfort of love,
if any fellowship of the Spirit,
if any affection and mercy,
fulfill my joy by being like-minded,
having the same love,
being of one accord, of one mind.

PHILIPPIANS 2:1-2

Special thanks to...

Michael Omartian; Chris, Paige, Scarlett, Juliette, and Victoria Omartian; Amanda and James Dallas West; Tom Vyskocil; Bob Hawkins, Kim Moore; Suzy Martinez; Roz Thompson; Susan Munao; and Patti Brussat for all your prayers, love, encouragement, and support. You are all the best.

With much love,

Stormie Omartian

Contents

Before You Begin...

After my husband, Michael, and I were first married, I found that praying together...out loud...in front of one another...was a little awkward. I was a new believer, and he had been a Christian for years before that time. So he had more experience with prayer than I did. We had met at a recording session several years before because I was a singer and he was a musician. I had been called to do this session by a good friend of mine, Terry, who I knew was a strong believer. And *I* knew that *she* knew I wasn't.

She was the recording contractor for many of the sessions I did, so I appreciated that she had mercy and not judgment toward me. At that particular session, Terry told me in advance that the session would be all Christian music, and I would be the only one there who was not a Christian. "But you will enjoy the people," she said.

She was right. I did.

All the people there—including engineers, musicians, singers, songwriters, the conductor, and the producer—were warm, kind, and welcoming. Because we were doing an entire album, the recording session was three days long, so I got to know the people on the session somewhat—especially Michael, the piano player. He and I talked on our breaks and lunch hours, and we realized we had many things in common. But once this session was over, we didn't meet any further because he was a believer and I wasn't. I'd heard he didn't want to date anyone who wasn't a Christian, and I wanted nothing to do with dating anyone who *was*. My mother always claimed, "*I* am child of God" as if no one else on earth was. And she could sound crazy at times when she talked about God. As it turned out, she was severely mentally ill, and she was physically and verbally abusive to me growing up, so I didn't want to marry anyone remotely like that.

The only reason I sort of knew what a believer was like was because Terry often talked to me about her church, her pastor, and her faith, and what it meant to receive Jesus as her Savior. I thought, *How nice that is...for her*. In fact, I thought, *This really works for these people. They are genuinely kind, and they all have a special spirit about them*.

Little did I know.

All of it was fascinating to me because I thought of myself as coming from a Christian family even though my mother only went to church Christmas Eve and Easter morning, and she was not consistent with that. My father always stayed home. He said he'd already had enough church to last a lifetime. Growing up, I thought that was all there was to being a Christian.

We had a huge family Bible that gathered dust in our living room, but it was never opened much that I know of, except for the few times I caught my mother reading it late at night. Every now and then I opened it myself, but I couldn't understand it. The last time I saw that Bible was when my mother angrily picked it up, went out the back door, and threw it in the backyard, where it landed in a muddy patch. I had just become a teenager, and I knew enough to not want to be in her way when she came back into the house. I ran to my room and kept very quiet the rest of the night. I never saw that Bible again, but when I came home from school the next day, it wasn't outside in the mud anymore.

Do You Find It Easy to Pray with Your Husband or Wife?

If you said yes to that question, that is a very good thing. It means you both have enough spiritual maturity and faith in God to believe He will hear your prayers and will answer. Not everyone has that.

About a year after I met Michael, Terry saw I wasn't doing well, so she took me to meet her pastor. I was open to what he told me—that if I received the Lord, He would change me from the inside out. This pastor said God had a purpose for my life, and He would help me find it. I had never heard anything like that before. So I received Jesus in his office. Terry was there with me, and she invited me to church that Sunday. I said yes.

I found it was a great and growing church that emphasized teaching people how to read and study the Bible consistently, how to worship God wholeheartedly, and how to pray powerfully and purposefully—not only on our own but also with other people. I also sensed the presence of love, peace, and joy in a way I had never experienced before, and it was palpable. It was real. I soon found out it was the presence of God.

Almost every time the church gathered for a service, 15 to 20 minutes was devoted to turning to two or three other people, joining hands and introducing ourselves by our first name, and then sharing a prayer request we wanted others to pray about for us. For example, "My name is Maria, and I would like prayer that I can find healing for my injured back." Or, "My name is Jason, and I would like prayer that I can find a better job."

They were simple requests and simple prayers, but those first circle times were difficult for me. Of course, if you had never done this before and didn't feel comfortable praying out loud, you could just say you were new at this and wanted to listen to the others pray this time. Still, you were encouraged to at least say what you wanted prayer for. But the more you were in those prayer circles, and the more you began to see answers to your prayer requests, the easier it became to be an active part of them. Your faith grew until you eventually felt able to pray for someone else.

As time went on, those once-dreaded prayer circles became something I looked forward to. In fact, on certain gatherings when there were several things that needed to take place during the church service, the pastor sometimes didn't have time for the prayer circles, and many of us were disappointed. For a number of us, that was the only time anyone ever prayed for us, and we felt sad when we missed this opportunity.

I saw Michael again when he started coming to this church, and not long after that we began dating. We were married about a year later. Michael and I started praying together at home, but I found that to be harder than I expected. It was because I needed to get over being concerned about whether I was praying as eloquently as the pastors did or like other people who were more experienced at it than I was. I had to understand that I was simply talking to God and did not need to impress anyone. I had to be honest with God about what I was seeking from Him, and to be grateful to know what He expected from me—honesty, humility, and love. He wanted me to have faith that He heard my prayers and would answer in *His way* and in *His time.*

I learned that praying is not telling God what to do. He knows what to do. But He wants us to come humbly before Him, communicating our love for Him, and then telling Him exactly what concerns our heart and what we would *like* Him to do.

All this is to say please do not feel uncomfortable or intimidated when praying with your husband or wife. No one is expecting you to sound like Billy Graham or Mother Teresa. Actually, there should never be any judgment on one another's prayers. There should be only gratefulness to God that you have a husband or wife who is willing to pray with you.

Think of it this way: Prayer is simply talking to God—humbly, honestly, respectfully, faithfully.

The more you and your spouse pray together, the more comfortable you will feel praying out loud with each other. When you pray the prayers in this book together, each prayer is already written out so you don't have to think of everything. And yes, those prayers count even if you haven't thought of them yourself. It's the same as when you sing a worship song someone else wrote. It's powerful for you as long as you believe the words you are singing or saying.

The prayers I have written for you both to pray are about subjects every couple needs to cover in their marriage. It can be hard to remember everything you need to pray about. These prayers can be complete in themselves, or they can be a starting point as you each continue praying about the specifics of your lives. And I pray you will do that.

The subjects in these chapters are not an assumption that you have these problems, but I'm assuming you never *want* these things to become a problem. Ask God to help both of you to be on the same page. Some couples may discover they are not only not on the same page—they feel they are not even in the same book. But God is the great unifier. He wants us to communicate so well with Him and together with our spouse that we grow in better understanding of each other. And rather than having a standoff over something, you can decide instead to stand together in prayer and ask God to help you find a meeting place—no matter what the subject is.

In order to be in the same book, you both need to make God's Word—the Holy Bible—the most important book you are in together and individually. It's important to be in agreement about His truth. Let *that* book, and this one, be a kind of insurance policy for your marriage. Divorce is expensive—in so many ways.

The truth is, you have a better chance of staying together if you pray together often. But we all want to not only *stay together* in our marriage. We also want to be *happy together*. In order to have all that, we need to be in agreement. That doesn't mean we are clones of one another. It means there are certain subjects we *do* agree on. And we can pray about the rest. We can pray that God will *help* us to have oneness and like-mindedness, having the same Lord and being of one accord and of one mind. Unity!

And He will.

CHAPTER 1

Maintaining a Right Heart

When you are first married, you have *soft* and *loving* hearts toward each other. (Otherwise, why get married?) So what can happen to change that? How do soft, loving hearts become separate or distant? How do they grow cold, hard, or indifferent? Where do things start to go wrong, and how can you prevent that from happening? I believe it's because we start to care *less* instead of caring *more* about each other. We neglect to *care fully* for our husband or wife. Instead, we appear to *care less*. Perhaps we don't notice how distracted we have become with our busy lives until we stop making our spouse a priority. Then unity of purpose is lost, and we grow apart and not together.

The good news is God has given us keys to unlock our hard hearts and open them back up to His love flowing through them. One of those keys is praying together in unity. Another is reading or hearing the Word of God. Jesus said, "I will give you the keys of the kingdom of heaven, and whatever you bind on earth will be bound in heaven, and whatever you loose on earth will be loosed in heaven" (Matthew 16:19). "Keys" here is talking about the authority Jesus gives in His name to believers who receive Him and love Him. We understand more and more about how the power to bind and loose is to be used as we pray and read His Word. In this instance we are talking about taking authority over our heart and maintaining it in a right way. It's about forbidding ourselves from even thinking an evil thought. When we pray like that, we can stop something bad from happening that we know shouldn't be. Or we can set ourselves free from some distraction that we have allowed to come into our life and take precedent over our relationship with our spouse. The sooner we pray about such things in unity, the quicker they can be corrected. Of course, wonderful distractions come into our lives that we must never neglect— such as children—that demand our time and focus. But we must make sure we don't neglect our husband or wife in the process of raising them. That will never work well.

If you or your husband or wife ever find yourself with a heart growing cold toward the other, remember that it starts with a heart that has already grown cold toward God. You can keep that from happening by praying together often and specifically asking God to keep your hearts soft toward Him as well as toward each other. The Bible says, "He who trusts in his own heart is a fool, but whoever walks wisely will be delivered" (Proverbs 28:26). God never sees the hardness of our heart as being okay. And if we allow it to become that way, it's our fault. We always have a choice. When we deliberately stay close to God in prayer, praise, and in His Word, His Holy Spirit in us keeps our heart soft toward Him and toward each other—if that is what we wholeheartedly desire.

Some of the other words the Bible uses to describe this unity are "being like-minded, having the same love, being of one accord," not being selfish or conceited, not thinking of ourselves more highly than the other, and not only looking out for our own interests. We must be looking out for our spouse's interests as well (see Philippians 2:1-4).

Pray that each of you will have a heart that is entirely open to God's truth and never open to the lies and enticements of the enemy of your marriage. Ask God to take away all pride in either of you if any arises because that always leads to a hardened heart. Remember that unity is always worth the effort it takes to work toward it. The two of you praying together in one accord will cause your prayers to be more powerful in their effect than you ever thought possible.

His Prayer

Lord, thank You for my wife. Thank You for Your love for her and for me. Teach us to love each other the way You love us. Thank You for putting a new heart and a new Spirit within us.

I pray You will always give me a heart that is soft toward my wife and take away any hardness of heart I have allowed to move into my thinking or feeling. Reveal any pride in me or anything I am not seeing in myself that does not please You. Help me to stay close to You because Your Spirit of love in me keeps me in line with Your will. Give each of us a heart that longs to know You better. Deepen our closeness to You as we pray together and live according to Your Word. Make us strong in faith, and give us ears to hear whatever You are speaking to us. Give each of us a *sound heart* because that brings new life (see Proverbs 14:30). If our hearts ever begin to grow distant or distracted, give each of us a *renewed* and *refreshed heart* of love for one another.

Thank You that You have given us the keys of Your kingdom of heaven so we can pray and stop things from happening that shouldn't be, or free ourselves from things we have allowed in our lives from which we want to be free. Teach us to use Your keys in prayer so that we will maintain a sound heart toward You and toward each other.

Lord, You have said that when we marry we leave our father and mother and form a new unity. Teach us to always remember that so we will make each other our greatest priority and form that unity You want between us.

In Jesus' name I pray.

Personal Prayer Needs

_____

_____

Her Prayer

Lord, I am grateful to You for my husband. Thank You that You brought us together for Your purpose. Teach us how to glorify You in the way we treat each other. Help us to bless You with how we bless each other. Thank You for calling us to be close to You, for that is our desire as well.

Lord, I pray that You would take away any hardness I have allowed to move into my heart. I know You never approve of that. I also know my heart and mind cannot be trusted to always have Your will in the center of them. Help my husband and me to pray together daily and to stay in Your Word so that we are fed with Your truth. Lead us by Your Spirit to obey You at all times and in every thought. Where either of us becomes selfish, wake us up to Your truth that any pride in our heart will lead us to a great fall. Teach us to daily look out for, and care for, one another.

Give both of us hearts that are continually renewed in Your Spirit so that we never allow ourselves to lose a right attitude toward You and Your ways. Keep us from assuming that our hearts are always right toward You and toward each other. Keep us from trusting in our own heart and becoming distracted away from You and each other. Help us to walk wisely so we will be delivered from that kind of creeping separation. Whenever it seems we are beginning to drift from one another in any way, give us a new heart and a new spirit within us as You have said in Your Word.

In Jesus' name I pray.

Personal Prayer Needs

_____

_____

TRUTH TO AGREE ON

Fulfill my joy by being like-minded,
having the same love, being of one accord, of one mind.
Let nothing be done through selfish ambition or conceit,
but in lowliness of mind let each esteem others
better than himself.
Let each of you look out not only for his own interests,
but also for the interests of others.

PHILIPPIANS 2:2-4

A man leaves father and mother,
and in marriage he becomes one flesh with a woman—
no longer two individuals, but forming a new unity.

MARK 10:7-9 MSG

The heart is deceitful above all things,
and desperately wicked; who can know it?

JEREMIAH 17:9

Let us not grow weary while doing good,
for in due season we shall reap if we do not lose heart.

GALATIANS 6:9

I will give you a new heart
and put a new spirit within you.

EZEKIEL 36:26

CHAPTER 2

Understanding the Power of Two

One of the best reasons to pray together with your husband or wife is because Jesus said, "Where two or three are gathered together in My name, I am there in the midst of them" (Matthew 18:20). In fact, that is one of the greatest promises in the Bible to you both, about which you would do well to be in absolute unity when you pray together. I am talking about just the two of you—husband and wife—praying together. God promises His presence will be with you when you do.

How great is that?

First of all, you need to understand that after you have made the commitment of marriage before God—and also your witnesses, family, and friends—God joins you together in such a powerful way that He sees you two as *one*. It's important to see yourselves the same way from that moment on as well. But just know that it doesn't happen overnight because it takes time to grow together. It takes praying together and being in unity about the important things. That doesn't mean either of you must deny who you are and become the other person. It just means both of you must ask the Lord to help you become more like *Him*.

God is the great unifier. With His help, He wants you to

communicate so well together that you understand each other. And rather than having an unhappy disagreement, you join together in prayer to ask God to enable you find a place of agreement no matter what the subject is. The power of two is great, but it's never more powerful than when you and your spouse pray together. Because God sees you two as one, your unity in prayer has special impact. As you agree together—especially about His Word—you become a great force in resisting the enemy's plans for you and your family. Don't ever doubt that.

By seeking that oneness in your relationship, you glorify God in your marriage. That does not mean you automatically agree on everything. It takes effort from both of you to pray that God will help you to become more like Him. And in order to find out what *He* is like, ask Him to show you. That not only takes prayer but also reading His Word—the Bible—separately and together. The more each of you read it, the more His likeness becomes etched in your heart and mind. When you read the Word of God, it strengthens your faith because "without faith it is impossible to please Him, for he who comes to God must believe that He is, and that He is a rewarder of those who diligently seek Him" (Hebrews 11:6).

Who doesn't want to please God?

The first thing to agree on is whom you are praying to. Decide if it is Mother Earth, your better self, a self-proclaimed god who did not lay down his life for you, or a god who is not always with you. If you are not praying to any of them, then you are better off agreeing to pray to your heavenly Father God, King of the universe, who created all things and gave His Son, Jesus, our Messiah, to be crucified on a cross. He was raised up on the third day and ascended into heaven to sit at the right hand of God to save, deliver, and transform anyone who believes in Him; to give them purpose; and receive them to spend eternity in heaven with Him. The Bible says, "If there is no resurrection of the dead, then Christ is not risen. And if Christ is not risen…your faith is futile; you are still in your sins!" (1 Corinthians 15:13-14, 17). If you don't agree on these things, your faith in Jesus and the power of two is futile until you come to unity of heart and mind about it. Work on that first. That is where your powerful oneness will be established.

If God wants you to be *one* with other *believers* in the body of Christ, why wouldn't He want you to be *one* with your *husband* or *wife*? He created you to be united together as one when you were married. Don't let anything separate you in mind, soul, or body and cause you to forget the power of two.

His Prayer

Thank You, Lord, that You have made my wife and me to be strong together in Your purpose for our lives. We worship You as our Lord and Savior, our strength against all that could tear us apart.

Lord, help me to strengthen my relationship with You so that our marriage will always be strong. Make me to be a peacemaker and keep me from stirring up strife in any way. Help my wife and me to remember we are always stronger together—especially when we pray together in unity and in the power of Your love. Lead us to become one just as You see us as a married couple. Teach us Your ways so we can walk in them. Give us great faith in Your Word. Enable us to believe that the two of us in unity are stronger than with any other bond.

Teach us to truly believe that when we pray together in Your name, that Your presence is there with us. You have provided everything we need to live the life You have for us. Help us to live without divisions, but rather to have the same mind. Not that we always think every thought the same, but that we believe the same way about the things that matter—especially about You and Your Ways. Help us to always be stronger together because we do everything with Your love in our hearts.

In Jesus' name I pray.

Personal Prayer Needs

_____

_____

Her Prayer

Lord, I thank You that You are a good God who never leaves us nor forsakes us. Thank You that when we draw near to You, You always draw near to us. Lord, help us to believe without doubt that whenever we agree together in prayer, Your presence is with us. That makes our prayers so powerful that nothing can prevail against them. We understand that the power of Your presence is far greater than anything we will ever face. For that reason alone, we pray You will help us to be like-minded, having unity of love for You and for one another. Teach us to always be of one accord and of one mind, and so fulfill Your will for us.

Enable us to understand the full power we have when we pray together in unity. Help us to agree on the truth of Your Word. Give us great faith to believe what You have said and what You have promised to us. Keep us from falling behind all You have for us because of doubt or fear. Draw us to diligently seek You with our whole heart and without any doubt that You are our one true God. You have said in Your Word that because we believe in You and have received You, Jesus, that each of us is a new creation. Old things have passed away and all things have become new. Thank You that because You have made us new, we don't have to live in the past or be weighed down by it, but we can rise above it together.

In Jesus' name I pray.

Personal Prayer Needs

_____

_____

TRUTH TO AGREE ON

If anyone is in Christ, he is a new creation;
old things have passed away;
behold, all things have become new.

2 Corinthians 5:17

…that you be perfectly joined together
in the same mind and in the same judgment.

1 Corinthians 1:10

Watch, stand fast in the faith,
be brave, be strong.
Let all that you do be done with love.

1 Corinthians 16:13-14

Two are better than one,
because they have a good reward for their labor.
For if they fall, one will lift up his companion.
But woe to him who is alone when he falls,
for he has no one to help him up.
Again, if two lie down together, they will keep warm;
but how can one be warm alone?

Ecclesiastes 4:9-11

CHAPTER 3

Enjoying the Freedom
of Forgiveness

When you decide to get married, you also must make a decision to be a forgiving person. That's because you will never be tested more on this than when you are married. But first, in order to forgive well, you need to receive *God's forgiveness* and understand how far-reaching that is. Receiving God's forgiveness makes it easier to forgive others, starting first with your husband or wife. Neither of you in a marriage can harbor unforgiveness toward the other because it is deadly to whoever hangs on to it. It will not only destroy you, but it will also destroy your mate and your marriage.

When Jesus was talking to His disciples about forgiving others, one of them asked Him if it was enough to forgive someone seven times. Jesus said to them that seventy times seven was more like it (see Matthew 18:21-22). That is 490 times if we are keeping count. In a marriage, we may have opportunities to forgive each other 490 times a week. But Jesus is not asking us to keep track of how many times we forgive. He is saying something more like, "As much as it takes." The thing is, Jesus has forgiven each of us far more than that. When we give *thanks* to *Him* for how much He has forgiven *us*, He gives us the heart and capacity to forgive others—especially our husband or wife. But we must *choose* to forgive.

Choosing to forgive *frees* us. *Not forgiving* the other person makes us miserable. That's because there is always a price to pay for unforgiveness. In fact, we can never get rid of the negative thoughts we have toward a person we have not forgiven. And when we have unforgiveness toward anyone, that affects our relationship with God. The Bible says, "Your iniquities have separated you from your God; and your sins have hidden His face from you, so that He will not hear" (Isaiah 59:2). Until you get rid of your lack of forgiveness, God is not going to listen to your prayers. That doesn't mean He *can't* hear your prayers. It means that He *won't* until you humbly confess sin before Him and invite Him to set you free of it. That instruction is too clear to even think about ignoring it.

Not forgiving your husband or wife is an *iniquity*. It is a *sin against God*. He feels that strongly about it. Jesus was crucified in order to bring *His* forgiveness to those who receive Him. So the least we can do for Him is forgive others—especially our *husband* or *wife*.

Most of the time we know when we have not forgiven someone. We feel it in our heart. But sometimes we can have unforgiveness in our heart and don't even realize it. That's why we must ask God to show us whether we have it or not. If we do, we must confess it to Him and ask Him to help us release it and be free of it. We have to be *willing* to forgive, but the good news is He will help us. There will be times when you must confess your unforgiveness to your spouse. Say that you don't want to feel that way, so would he or she pray with you about it?

Forgiving someone frees you from the torture that *not forgiving* brings. Sometimes forgiving doesn't come easy because the offense is great. When that happens, ask God to help you. He understands when an offense is so grievous that you don't want to let someone off the hook. But *forgiveness doesn't make the other person right, it makes you free*. I have said this in my other books about marriage because I had to learn this as a nonnegotiable truth if I wanted to move on in my life. God is not looking for you to get even. He wants you to get free so you won't get stuck in unforgiveness hell. "He who follows righteousness and mercy finds life, righteousness, and honor" (Proverbs 21:21).

Because many opportunities for unforgiveness are in a marriage, you must keep the communication lines open. This is too important to not pray about it. Keep asking God to show you when you need to forgive *anyone*, but especially your *husband* or *wife*. Unforgiveness shows on everyone's face who has it. People will sense that in you even if they don't know exactly what it is. And it will definitely be evident to your spouse because it will come out in your attitude.

It's not worth it to let unforgiveness grow and fester. The more it exists, the more destruction it will do—in your relationship and in your body.

His Prayer

Lord, thank You for forgiving us of all our transgressions and giving us a new beginning. Because we have received You into our hearts, Your forgiveness of all past sins is complete. Thank You that when we ask, You will reveal to us when we either need to forgive or ask for forgiveness.

Help us to always freely forgive each other quickly so we never allow any kind of resentment to build up between us. Give us each a heart of mercy toward the other in the exact way You extend mercy toward both of us. You have said in Your Word that You are "merciful and gracious, slow to anger, and abounding in mercy" (Psalm 103:8). Help us to be that way too. Teach us to always live Your way. Enable us to be righteous and merciful toward each other at all times. Thank You that Your forgiveness is extended to us whenever we come humbly to You and seek it.

Teach us to communicate well with each other so that we do not miscommunicate with words that are hurtful. Help us to always be as Your Word says, "Bearing with one another, and forgiving one another, if anyone has a complaint against another; even as Christ forgave you, so you also must do. But above all these things put on love, which is the bond of perfection" (Colossians 3:13-14). Your Word makes it clear that Your love is unconditional and it perfects us. May our love for each other always be readily available and easily seen.

In Jesus' name I pray.

Personal Prayer Needs

_____

_____

Her Prayer

Lord, thank You for always forgiving us when we come to You humbly and confess our sins and faults. Thank You that You will help us to do the same for each other. Show us whenever we have any lack of forgiveness between us. Reveal to us now if there is anything that needs to be brought to light so resentment does not build up in either of us. Keep us from ever allowing ourselves to live in a prison of unforgiveness that can erect walls between us. Enable each of us to have a heart that is always filled with mercy and a willingness to forgive. Thank You that Your mercy toward us is everlasting (see Psalm 100:5). Enable us to be more like You in every way.

We know that to be truly free to become more like You means we must separate ourselves from anything that separates us from You. One of the things we need to stay clear of is not forgiving each other *quickly*. We know that puts up a barrier between us and You, and we cannot bear that.

Cause forgiveness to flow like a river between us so we don't become unkind. You have said that if we are praying in Your name and we realize that we need to forgive anyone, we must do that right away. That is so You will not withhold Your forgiveness from us (see Mark 11:25). That is a miserable consequence we must always keep in mind when we are struggling to forgive.

In Jesus' name I pray.

Personal Prayer Needs

_____

_____

TRUTH TO AGREE ON

Be kind to one another, tenderhearted, forgiving one another,
even as God in Christ forgave you.

EPHESIANS 4:32

If you forgive men their trespasses,
your heavenly Father will also forgive you.
But if you do not forgive men their trespasses,
neither will your Father forgive your trespasses.

MATTHEW 6:14-15

As far as the east is from the west,
so far has He removed our transgressions from us.

PSALM 103:12

Stand fast therefore in the liberty by which Christ
has made us free, and do not be entangled again
with a yoke of bondage.

GALATIANS 5:1

As the elect of God, holy and beloved, put on tender mercies,
kindness, humility, meekness, longsuffering;
bearing with one another, and forgiving one another,
if anyone has a complaint against another;
even as Christ forgave you, so you also must do.
But above all these things put on love, which is the bond of
perfection. And let the peace of God rule in your hearts,
to which also you were called in one body; and be thankful.

COLOSSIANS 3:12-15

CHAPTER 4

Knowing When Something Needs to Change

I f prayer is simply talking to God, then one of the *purest* forms of prayer is worship and praise to Him. Worship causes us to focus our heart and mind on God and away from ourselves. When we reach up to Him with our whole heart in praise, He reaches out to touch us with all that He is. Even though our praise and worship are all about Him, He pours out on us our greatest blessings at the same time.

The Bible says of the Lord, "You are holy, enthroned in the praises of Israel" (Psalm 22:3). When we praise and worship God, His presence lives in our worship—in our words and our songs. That's why you can expect to sense His presence when you worship Him. And worshipping Him together as a married couple is the most powerful thing you can do. There will always be power in that unity.

So when you need to feel a sense of God's presence with you, the quickest, most powerful, and most effective way to have that is to stop everything you are doing and give praise and thanks to God for who He is and all He has done for you. Whenever you feel the need for something to change—in your attitude, mind, circumstances, or communication—this is exactly what you need to do.

The reason praise and worship make such an enormous difference when a husband and wife praise and worship God together is because when you are in the presence of God, things change. Always! Your mind can change. Your situation can change. Your attitude can change. Even your heart can change. When you know that something needs to change but you are not certain how to make that happen yourself, just know you will not be able to do it alone. At least not to the degree that God can work that in you. You need the presence of God—plus your *unity, oneness* of *mind,* and *purpose* together as a couple—in order to move powerfully into that kind of holy breakthrough.

If you ever come to an impasse between the two of you and can't seem to make a change, deliberately worship God together and invite Him to inhabit your praises. You will sense a stronghold breaking that cannot withstand the power of His powerful presence. You will feel it—if not at that very moment, then soon. You were born to worship God, and the quicker you do it as your greatest privilege and joy, the clearer you will sense His deeper purpose for your lives—individually and together.

One of the most amazing things about God is that He shares Himself with us. When we lift up our hearts to Him in worship, we are closer to Him than at any other time. And He pours into us His love, joy, peace, and all the other fruits of His Spirit. He even shares His power with us. It's not that we become as powerful as He is. It's that we can move more powerfully in our faith and prayers than we could ever begin to do without Him being poured into us.

Remember, when you can't see a way to change anything, *He* can. And He can impart that change to you at that moment or perhaps later when you are least expecting it.

God always hears a worshipper (see John 9:31). That's a good thing when you know you need something to change. It could be because of something you or your husband or wife has done wrong. Or it could be because of something you both have done right. Sometimes the hard things you are going through are because of the work of the enemy trying to thwart the plans of God in your life. Whatever it is, God will show you as you lift your heart to Him in worship. The quickest way to break through something that needs to change is to praise God as long as it takes to sense the breakthrough you need. Never underestimate the power of heartfelt praise and worship to God from a husband and wife together.

His Prayer

Lord, we worship You for all that You are. You are our heavenly Father, and You know all that we need even before we ask. Thank You that when we seek You, You are our God who can be found. When we praise You for sharing Yourself with us, we are always richer for it. Thank You for sharing Your love with us because You are *love*. You share Your power because You are *all-powerful*. You share Your *wisdom* because You are *all-knowing*. You share Your *presence* because You are "*God with us*." Thank You that the more we worship You, the more we know You and become like You.

We lift You up in worship and praise because You are our almighty God for whom nothing is impossible. Thank You that nothing is too hard for You. You are my help, and I will hide myself in You. I praise You for all that You are. You are able to do "exceedingly above all that we ask or think, according to Your *power* that *works in* us" (Ephesians 3:20). Thank You that Your power is always working in us because we worship only You. We express our love to You with everything that is in us. We want to always do Your will. Help us to never neglect our times of worship and praise for You because we appreciate who You are and all You have done for us. We praise You for all You are doing and will do in our lives.

In Jesus' name I pray.

Personal Prayer Needs

_____

_____

Her Prayer

Lord, I thank You that You are our God of love, peace, and joy. You loved me and my husband before we even knew You. Thank You for Your love that is poured out *on* us, *in* us, and *through* us. We are grateful to You because Your love for us will never end. You are everlasting, and so Your love for us will never fail. Thank You that Your love for us is unconditional. We worship You for Your salvation, deliverance, and transformation. Your grace and mercy toward us never come to an end. We worship You for Your life-changing, mountain-moving power in our lives. Thank You for enabling us to do Your will and showing us how to glorify You.

We worship You for Your unfailing provision toward us. You have said in Your Word that You, our heavenly Father, know the things we need before we even ask (see Matthew 6:8). Thank You that Your resurrection power that raised Jesus from the dead will also raise us when we die so we will live in heaven with You for eternity. We praise You for all Your great promises to us. Thank You for changing us and our circumstances every time we worship You. Help us to remember that You are greater than anything we may face at any time in our lives. Your Word says that when we worship You and do Your will, You hear our prayers (see John 9:31). We desire to worship You always and do only Your will forever.

In Jesus' name I pray.

Personal Prayer Needs

_____

_____

TRUTH TO AGREE ON

I will praise You, O LORD, with my whole heart;
I will tell of all Your marvelous works.
I will be glad and rejoice in You;
I will sing praise to Your name, O Most High.

PSALM 9:1-2

You shall love the LORD your God with all your heart,
with all your soul, and with all your mind.

MATTHEW 22:37

We know that God does not hear sinners;
but if anyone is a worshiper of God
and does His will, He hears him.

JOHN 9:31

To Him who is able to do exceedingly abundantly
above all that we ask or think,
according to the power that works in us,
to Him be glory...forever and ever.

EPHESIANS 3:20-21

The eyes of the LORD run to and fro
throughout the whole earth,
to show Himself strong on behalf of those
whose heart is loyal to Him.

2 CHRONICLES 16:9

CHAPTER 5

Agreeing on the Way You Handle Money

One of the most important things to agree on in your marriage is how you handle your money. How is your money earned? How is it spent? How much do you give to God? How much do you save? What is the plan for your future? It's better to have a plan than winging it and hoping things work out. It's important that all these things be prayed about and agreed upon. This can be complicated if one spouse is a saver and the one is a spender in the extreme. But God will always help you figure your finances out as you both seek Him about these things. And it can be done. No one needs to be a dictator, but you do have to come to some kind of agreement.

God promises to "supply all our needs" according to His riches (see Philippians 4:18-19). He has riches in abundance, and when we seek Him about how we are to gain our money, how to spend it, and how to give to others, He will give us specific guidance.

One of the worst pressures on a marriage is having financial problems. And the longer the problems go on, the greater the pressure becomes. It's important to do whatever is necessary to stay debt-free. You must plan ahead carefully so that you don't get in over your heads. Not having enough money to pay the bills is always scary, and the feeling of drowning in debt is never sustainable for long. Living within your means and paying your bills, while being able to save for emergencies, is the bare minimum you must do. Countless marriages have been destroyed because of unbearable financial struggles.

It's important to regularly pray about this as a couple. Ask God to help you both be of one mind regarding your finances. Having a strong sense of unity about this keeps you from fearing the worst. If one of you works hard to bring in money, and the other spends more than is being made, that will give you both a feeling of hopelessness. It causes doubt about the future of your relationship if you can't figure out how to agree.

The Bible says, "The blessing of the LORD makes one rich, and He adds no sorrow with it" (Proverbs 10:22). When you put the Lord in charge of your finances—together with your spouse—God will *guide you* and *bless them.* The Bible also says, "Those who seek the LORD shall not lack any good thing" (Psalm 34:10). This is a major truth to agree on and remember.

Another thing we need to pray about is this: "Let the beauty of the LORD our God be upon us, and establish the work of our hands for us; yes, establish the work of our hands" (Psalm 90:17). Asking God to establish you in your work is powerful—especially so when you pray together about that. Everyone has work to do. If both of you are working, but only one of you is working for money, the one who is not getting paid is still working. Whether it's raising children, taking care of a home, taking care of animals or a garden or a farm, or creating something, it's still important work and definitely worth praying for and seeking God's blessings.

A husband and wife have to agree on the best way to manage their finances. It's such an important part of your marriage that you must keep it covered in prayer. Even when things are going well, everything can change in an instant. Decide together—with the guidance of God—how to save, spend, give, and invest. If you are in a difficult place right now regarding your finances, stop immediately and praise God because He promises to give you everything you need and bless all you have if you submit all You have to Him.

The key here is asking God to be in charge of your finances and then asking Him to bless the work that you do. Make this an ongoing prayer for you together, and it will keep you away from financial trouble. God will bless you with provision as you submit your finances to Him.

His Prayer

Lord, I thank You that You are our provider. Thank You for providing for all our needs. I pray you will give to both my wife and me the wisdom we need concerning our finances. Help us to make sound decisions regarding how we earn money and the way we spend it. Help us to always seek You first—and each other—before we make any major decisions. Thank You that You will provide everything we need when we put You first.

Open the doors necessary for us to find good work for both of us. Help us to make excellent decisions as to what our work will be. Show us how to spend our money wisely. Lead us by Your Spirit in all we do, but especially regarding finances at all times. Teach us to communicate openly about money matters. Where we have debt that is burdensome, show us how to become free of it. If we are not doing what You would have for us, open doors to us for finding better work. Show us what we should be doing.

Always reveal to us how to give to You and others as You would have us to do. You have said in Your Word that Your blessings bring riches and You add no sorrow to them (see Proverbs 10:22). Thank You that You know what we need before we ask. Help us remember that You want us to ask according to Your will.

In Jesus' name I pray.

Personal Prayer Needs

_____

_____

Her Prayer

Lord, I pray You will guide us as to how our finances are earned, spent, saved, given, and invested. Keep us from living in a dreamland in any way regarding our finances. Enable us to have similar goals and to be able to come to an agreement as to how we handle our finances. Help us to avoid the financial pitfalls that are common in a marriage, and enable us to have good communication between us. Teach us to always be on the same side and able to work things out peacefully together in unity.

Help us to seek Your kingdom first in all things, but especially with regard to our finances. Show us how to plan well so we always live within our means. Teach us how to develop our skills and gifts so we will do good work and be paid fairly for the work we do. Give us wisdom in handling all that You provide for us, and teach us to be good stewards of everything You give us. Help us to plan carefully and calmly for the future and yet always be able to help others as You reveal to us their needs. We submit our money and goods to You because we know that all good things come from You. You have said in Your Word that when we seek You first, all we need will come to us (Matthew 6:33). Help us to always seek You first—especially with regard to our finances.

In Jesus' name I pray.

Personal Prayer Needs

_____

_____

TRUTH TO AGREE ON

Whatever you do, do it heartily,
as to the Lord and not to men.

COLOSSIANS 3:23

Lay up for yourselves treasures in heaven,
where neither moth nor rust destroys
and where thieves do not break in and steal.

MATTHEW 6:20

He who has a slack hand becomes poor,
but the hand of the diligent makes rich.
He who gathers in summer is a wise son;
he who sleeps in harvest is a son who causes shame.

PROVERBS 10:4-5

Whoever shuts his ears to the cry of the poor
will also cry himself and not be heard.

PROVERBS 21:13

My God shall supply all your need
according to His riches in glory by Christ Jesus.

PHILIPPIANS 4:19

CHAPTER 6

Learning to Love like God

When we get married, we are positive we will love one another forever. We are certain we have that part down. We think, *No problem. Got it.* And this is true at least for the first year or two or three of married life. But what about the fifth year? Or the seventh? Tenth? Fifteenth? Twentieth? Thirtieth? And beyond? The Bible says, "If we love one another, God abides in us, and His love has been perfected in us" (1 John 4:12). It also says, "Whoever confesses that Jesus is the Son of God, God abides in him, and he in God...God is love, and he who abides in love abides in God, and God in him" (1 John 4:15-16).

Can we promise to always love one another like *God loves* us without *God's* love being *in* us? I don't think we can. We need His love to be renewed in us every day. It's not that *His* love dissipates in us. It's *we* who *fail* to *renew* it from our end. The way we do that is by praying to our God of love and inviting Him to fill us afresh with His love every day. It happens also by reading His Word and allowing it to strengthen our faith as God promises it will do.

It's all about developing your personal relationship with God. If your relationship with Him is weak, your marriage relationship will be weakened as well. When you are open to receiving more of God's love in you, you will grow in love for your mate. It is an automatic blessing that your love for God—and God's love *in you*—will always overflow from *your* heart to your husband or wife.

You can have a great marriage if you and your spouse pray for each other. That's because prayer can change everything. The more you seek God in your individual relationship with Him—as well as together as a couple—the more you will sense God's presence when you agree together in prayer.

Keep in mind that your husband or wife cannot fulfill your every need. That's why God wants you to come to Him alone, to be certain you have faith that He *can* and *will* meet the *needs you* have.

We are all selfish enough to want what we want from our marriage, and those expectations can seem overwhelming to the spouse who is trying to meet all the hopes of the other. However, it will never be acceptable for a husband or wife to be rude, uncaring, disrespectful, or abusive while demanding to get his or her needs met. God does not look kindly on that. Of course, certain expectations need to be met, such as basic kindness and physical intimacy. Ask God to help you and your mate to be on the same page regarding this important part of your life together.

The Bible says you are made in God's image. God said, "Let Us make man in Our image, according to Our likeness" (Genesis 1:26). Isn't it amazing that you and your spouse are made in the image of God? You need to always value that in yourself and with each other.

When someone asked Jesus, "Which is the first commandment of all?" Jesus answered him, saying, "'You shall love the LORD your God with all your heart, with all your soul, with all your mind, and with all your strength.' This is the first commandment. And the second, like it, is this: 'You shall love your neighbor as yourself.' There is no other commandment greater than these" (Mark 12:28, 30-31). Keep in mind that your closest neighbor is your husband or wife. It doesn't get any clearer—or closer. How can we live in unity if we don't have love for each other in our marriage?

The more we grow in knowledge of who God is, the more we will become like Him. The more we grow in love with Jesus and come to understand how much He loves us, the more we will welcome Him to pour His love into us. And our greater knowledge of God and our expanding love for Jesus will increase our ability, capacity, and desire to pour our love into others—our spouse and children first.

Unity doesn't mean you agree on everything. It means you agree on the most important things—God's Word and His ways. You agree on the truth. You agree on what is right. Ask God to help you to truly love your husband or wife the way He loves you. We all definitely need His help in order to do that.

His Prayer

Lord, thank You that Your love for us is unconditional and unfailing. Thank You for pouring Your love on us and enabling us to love each other more than we ever knew we could.

Help my wife and me to love each other the way You love us. Teach us to care for one another in ways that please You. Your Word says, "I am persuaded that neither *death* nor *life*, nor *angels* nor *principalities* nor *powers*, nor *things present* nor *things to come*, nor *height* nor *depth*, nor any other *created thing*, shall be able to *separate* us from the *love* of *God* which is in Christ Jesus our Lord" (Romans 8:38-39). We cannot separate ourselves from God's promise to love us. Help us to always fully agree on that.

Build in us the kind of love for each other that You have for us—the kind that never fails, and that doesn't allow anything to get in the way of it. Keep us mindful of the enemy's desire to destroy our marriage, and help us take deliberate steps to avoid all temptation to believe his lies. Keep us aware of anyone or anything that attempts to creep in and tries to undermine what our greater priority is to one another. We know that love is of You, Lord, because You *are* love. And Your love in us will always keep us in love with one another. Help us to understand what we can expect of each other, and what the expectations are we should clearly put in You.

In Jesus' name I pray.

Personal Prayer Needs

_____

_____

Her Prayer

Lord, I thank You that nothing can ever separate us from Your love. Your love for us is so deep that it is without end. Your love is there for us in difficult times, and it will get us through them or lift us above them. Your love is unconditional. You never stop loving us, whether we feel we deserve it or not.

I pray for my husband and me to always have the kind of love that refuses to let anything or anyone come between us. Let us never want to get even or hurt one another because of some perceived failure on either of our parts. Help us to recognize a setup by the enemy of our souls to destroy our marriage. Open our eyes to see the truth so we are not vulnerable to anything that is not right in Your eyes. Help us to see with great clarity where we have invited—or been open to—anything that gives the impression of evil. If anyone or any influence ever seeks to come between us in any way, remove that person or influence from our lives. Show us any place we have expectations of one another when we should put our expectations in You and not pressure each other to meet our every need. We can expect of one another love, kindness, care, support, help, comfort, communication, honesty, compassion, physical and emotional intimacy, and general decency. Help us to agree together to love each other in those ways no matter what happens because it is the right thing to do. We ask that You, Lord, would teach us about Your love in ways we will never forget so that we love each other in ways that bless You.

In Jesus' name I pray.

Personal Prayer Needs

_____

_____

TRUTH TO AGREE ON

Beloved, let us love one another, for love is of God;
and everyone who loves is born of God and knows God.
He who does not love does not know God, for God is love.

1 JOHN 4:7-8

A new commandment I give to you,
that you love one another; as I have loved you,
that you also love one another.
By this all will know that you are My disciples,
if you have love for one another.

JOHN 13:34-35

In this is love, not that we loved God, but that He loved us
and sent His Son to be the propitiation for our sins.
Beloved, if God so loved us, we also ought to love one another.
No one has seen God at any time. If we love one another,
God abides in us, and His love has been perfected in us.

1 JOHN 4:10-12

God is love, and he who abides in love
abides in God, and God in him.

1 JOHN 4:16

CHAPTER 7

Watching What You Say

The Bible talks a great deal about unity in the way we speak. This is extremely important to God, especially for a married couple. Jesus said He wants us to be unified just as God, Jesus, and the Holy Spirit are one because if we do that, we will be perfect (see John 17:20-23). And surely we realize there is no way we can be perfect on our own. We can only *pray* that God will work *His* perfection *in* us. Initially, we have to believe it is possible. Then we have to want it enough to pray consistently about it.

The first thing we must do is limit our complaints. The Bible says *we* shouldn't "complain, as some of them also complained, and were destroyed by the destroyer" (1 Corinthians 10:10). Obviously, the consequences can be very steep when we complain.

In a marriage, complaining not only destroys the complainer, but it also destroys the other person and possibly the marriage. That's because it is a heavy burden to carry every day. No matter who the complainer is, it is exhausting. It's good to share your complaint with your spouse for the purpose of praying about it, but not to be finger-pointing and blaming one another. After you have prayed about it, at some point you must believe God has heard your request and you leave the matter in His hands.

So cease complaining and thank God that He has the ability to change things.

Being married gives you the perfect practice ground of opportunities for watching what you say. This is the best place to cultivate that attitude of oneness and unity. That doesn't mean you always have to agree on everything, but you have to want to find that important common ground of what you *do* agree on. Search for the most important issues, such as who *God* is and what He requires of you. Also, what *Jesus* has done for you and all He has given to you. Agree that the *Bible* is the inspired *Word* of *God,* and it can change your heart and mind for the better every time you read it or hear it.

The Bible says, "May the God of *patience* and *comfort,* grant you to be *like-minded* toward one another, according to Christ Jesus, that you may with *one mind* and *one mouth* glorify the God and Father of our Lord Jesus Christ. Therefore receive one another, just as Christ also received us, to the glory of God" (Romans 15:5-7). "To receive one another" is a way of life that glorifies God. It pleases God, and that is always good for a marriage.

These words in Romans 15 are for the entire Christian community, but this passage of Scripture is often used as a wedding text because it describes what a marriage *should* be like—the way a marriage should operate. We are to mercifully receive our spouse the way Jesus receives us. Jesus is our role model. And the words in these verses above describe how a husband and wife should be toward one another. When Jesus received us, He accepted us. We should ask God to help us accept each other. We are on the same team. We are not in competition with each other. We don't have to fight with one another.

What you have in your heart will come out of your mouth (see Matthew 12:34). That is why it is important to make sure your heart is filled with God's love, peace, and joy *before* you speak.

When there comes a time that you need to speak to your spouse about something that may be hard for him or her to hear, pray *before* you speak. Ask God to show you what you should say and how to say it. Ask Him to prepare the heart of your spouse so he or she will open their heart to hear what you are saying. Speaking something that may hurt the other can be tempered greatly by the love of God in your heart.

The Bible says, "The kingdom of God is not in word but in power" (1 Corinthians 4:20). It's not *our* words but *God's power* behind the words that we speak—or that God gives us to speak—that enables us to speak truthful, powerful, and soul-healing words.

The Bible also says, "*Speak the same thing*, and that there *be no divisions* among you" (1 Corinthians 1:10). Speaking the same thing means there should not be major divisions between you and your spouse that cannot be smoothed out in prayer.

His Prayer

Lord, thank You that we can go to You for anything—even for the right words and attitudes we need in order to speak to our spouse in a healing and building manner.

My wife and I especially need Your help in order to watch what we say to one another so that we don't develop a growing list of hurts, offenses, or resentments that can build up over time. Teach us to pray *before* we say things that may be hard for the other to hear. Help us to always remember that we have the mind of Christ. I know You are asking us to be unified, while still keeping in mind that each of us has distinctive gifts, talents, and other valuable assets to offer to the other. Give us eyes to see those in each other and appreciate them. Enable us to recognize when we are complaining more than praying and trusting You to answer those prayers. Teach us when we pray about such matters to leave them in Your hands and be thankful that You have the ability to change things.

Your Word says that we have the power to speak words that bring life or death to each other and to our situations. Help us to always be mindful of that so we will speak to each other in a way that builds up and brings life. We trust You to help us control our words so we don't do damage to the heart of the other.

In Jesus' name I pray.

Personal Prayer Needs

_____

_____

Her Prayer

Lord, Your Word says that life and death are found in the power of the words we say (see Proverbs 18:21). We need Your help in order to make certain that we always speak life to one another, even when we need to speak words that are hard to hear.

Specifically, help my husband and me to appreciate the qualities in each other that are the greatest blessings in our relationship. Teach us to not only have *time for one another,* but also that individually we need to *make time for You* as well. Help us to present our hearts, minds, souls, and bodies to You so we can understand how we can grow to be more like You. We want to come to You to sense Your presence in our lives, knowing that every time we do, we are changed in some way. The most certain way to become more like You is to praise You for all we know of You. Every time we do that, You pour into us more of Yourself—more of Your love, peace, joy, power, goodness, and other perfect qualities. The more we become like You, the easier it is to be gracious and kind to one another in a way that is pleasing to You.

Help us to speak words to each other that build up, comfort, heal, encourage, and bring life to one another. I know we may not be able to immediately agree on everything, but help us to find a place of solid unity in the most important things. Reveal to us clearly when either of us has become a complainer so we will not set ourselves up for any kind of destruction.

In Jesus' name I pray.

Personal Prayer Needs

_____

_____

TRUTH TO AGREE ON

How good and pleasant it is
when God's people live together in unity!
Psalm 133:1 niv

I plead with you, brethren,
by the name of our Lord Jesus Christ,
that you all speak the same thing,
and that there be no divisions among you.
1 Corinthians 1:10

Out of the abundance of the heart the mouth speaks.
Matthew 12:34

"Who has known the mind of the Lord
that he may instruct Him?"
But we have the mind of Christ.
1 Corinthians 2:16

Death and life are in the power of the tongue,
And those who love it will eat its fruit.
Proverbs 18:21

CHAPTER 8

Choosing Your Friends Carefully

The Bible says, "He who walks with wise men will be wise, but the companion of fools will be destroyed" (Proverbs 13:20). The consequences of spending time with people who are short on godly wisdom is clear. It's too easy to be led astray by people—even Christians—who have themselves been led off the path of the Lord's will by evil people. So be careful of the friends you keep. Be quick to give up evil company when you see it. Do not hang around with people who corrupt your character. Sometimes you can't see it clearly yourself, but your spouse clearly can. That's why you must choose your friends wisely and receive your spouse's opinions, even if they sometimes don't align with yours.

Where there is disagreement between you regarding the company you keep, ask God to show you if the relationship in question is God ordained. Hold it up to the light of the Lord to see if the influence on you or your spouse is good, positive, right, and God glorifying or if it is negative, disturbing, or unhealthy. Are you or your spouse influenced in a bad way by this person who is not at all inspiring or uplifting? In the presence of that person, do you become depressed, sad, anxious, unbelieving, or arrogant and drawn to activity that is not right or good?

Ask yourself whether this person is a good influence on you or your spouse. Do you see good traits coming from yourself—or your husband or wife—when either of you spend time with this person?

If a person has too much influence on you or your spouse that is not God glorifying, the Bible says, "Put away from yourselves the evil person" (1 Corinthians 5:13). Pray about that. God did not say you could never be around anyone who wasn't perfect in His eyes, but the people you are most often around should be the ones who have the greatest influence in your life. They must be godly.

One of the most important things to realize is that if someone you claim to be your friend is a person your spouse cannot tolerate, carefully consider that your spouse may be judging this friend by how you behave around them. If a friend of yours causes you to have a different personality—or do things that are not godly or right when you are with them—allow your spouse to explain what he or she sees, feels, or senses whenever you spend time with that person. Ask God to show you if that is the best person to be your close friend and greatest influence. God will do that. Take heed to what He shows you. Be willing to let anyone who leads you away from the things of God to find another friendship. If either of you cannot imagine a life without this person, ask God to show you why. He will.

These days it's not hard to come up against an evil person who inserts a bad influence in your life if you are not very careful and watchful. And you may not really catch it because you are not like that yourself. For example, you can be easily influenced by the dark side of today's culture without realizing it. Ask God to help you both see the truth about people you meet. Pray about everyone who comes into your life with any kind of influence. Jesus was with His disciples for three years teaching them about evil people, but He still had to pray for their faith to not fail in the midst of Satanic influence (see Luke 22:31-32). How much more do you need to pray for yourself and your spouse to not be deceived by friendly people who don't have godly motives toward you?

If your spouse voices some concern about a person you are being too easily influenced by, pray with your spouse about this. They may be aware of something you are not. And perhaps they have already prayed about it, and God has revealed something that would be good for you to consider. It's definitely not worth sacrificing the quality of your marriage on that battleground.

His Prayer

Lord, we declare You to be Lord over our lives. Teach us to surrender ourselves to You each day so we can be in unity about our love and devotion to You and to each other in a way that grows deeper each time we pray.

Help us to have good, godly friends who influence us to have a deeper and better relationship with You and with each other. Give us wisdom to recognize anyone in our lives whom we allow to influence us but is not the best person for that. If either of us spends a great amount of time with someone who influences us to question Your ways, or to be critical of our spouse, or in any other way is not a positive influence on us, give us eyes to see that. We want to always ask You if this friend is someone You have brought into our lives for Your purposes.

Give us a strong sense of anyone who is a bad influence in our lives who does not encourage us to walk closer to You and to each other. If we find the people we trust most, and see most often, have a negative influence on us, help us to stand strong and not allow them to be the dominant influence in our lives. Open our eyes to not be blind to the true character of others. Teach us to not allow the people we work with most closely, or spend the most time with, to pull us away from Your teachings and ways. We never want to be guilty of allowing bad influences to dominate our lives or undermine our marriage.

In Jesus' name I pray.

Personal Prayer Needs

_____

_____

Her Prayer

Thank You, Lord, that You have made us to have friends, but not at the sacrifice of our marriage. I pray that my husband and I will always be guided by You concerning the friendships we keep. Help us to maintain good, godly friends as our closest and most influential relationships. We never want relationships that cause us to become more distant from You, Your ways, or from one another. Open our eyes to see the truth about people and not be led astray. Keep us both from ever being led in the way of evil by anyone. Protect us from the influence of anyone who is ungodly in heart and mind. Teach us to always "walk in the light" as You are in the light (see 1 John 1:7). Keep us in agreement about that.

Whenever one or both of us stray from the path You have for us, and we recognize a bad influence in our lives, give us the ability to talk to one another about this and have open ears to hear the truth. Open our eyes also to see what You clearly want us to understand. Help us to talk about our friends and share what we truly feel about them. Keep us from ever making our spouse feel that any friends we have are more important to us than he or she is. Let us never make idols out of our friends to the diminishment of our spouse. Give us eyes to see how we are affected by each of our friends' presence in our lives. If either of us has a serious complaint about a relationship the other has, give each of us the strength to hear the truth. We want to be influenced by You, Lord, and not the flattery of others.

In Jesus' name I pray.

Personal Prayer Needs

_____

_____

TRUTH TO AGREE ON

Do not be deceived: "Evil company corrupts good habits."
1 Corinthians 15:33

I am a companion of all who fear You,
and of those who keep Your precepts.

Psalm 119:63

Do not be unequally yoked together with unbelievers.
For what fellowship has righteousness with lawlessness?
And what communion has light with darkness?

2 Corinthians 6:14

Do not enter the path of the wicked,
and do not walk in the way of evil.

Proverbs 4:14

I have written to you not to keep company
with anyone named a brother,
who is sexually immoral, or covetous, or an idolater,
or a reviler, or a drunkard, or an extortioner—
not even to eat with such a person.

1 Corinthians 5:11

CHAPTER 9

Resisting the Enemy

When you and your spouse are in complete unity about the things that truly matter most, you will also be unified in opposition against the horrific evil you see in the world. You two will always be united in the things of the world you pray against. You will want to stand together against everything that grieves God so you can pray together in power about them.

One of the things you must realize as a married person is that you two have an enemy. This is God's enemy also. If you have the light of the Lord in you, the enemy sees that, but keep in mind that his power is limited. This is especially true next to the almighty power of the Lord God of the universe who watches over you, and who will never leave you nor forsake you.

The enemy does not like your marriage. He wants to see it destroyed and your children captured by his own evil tactics. But we are able to stand strong against this evil takeover by being in agreement about the ways of God and resisting all the enemy's plans. When you serve God and only God and give no place to the enemy—when you worship your heavenly Father, who created and loves you; His Son, Jesus, who saved, healed, delivered, and restored you; and His Holy Spirit, who leads, guides, and comforts you—then no one else can ever take the place of God in your heart.

One of the strongest factors in your stance of resistance toward the enemy is your ability to stand in unity of faith, prayer, praise, and the power of God's Word. When you have all that, nothing can oppose you with any degree of success. Most people have no idea of the strength of the power of God on their behalf. Too many people do not believe that God is able to protect them from evil. Praise God that we can put our trust in Him to keep us safe.

All serious believers in Jesus are in a war between God and His enemy. But even if you are not a believer, you are still in the war. You just don't know it yet. Many believers are in the war, but they don't understand it. They can get knocked down, but they think bad things happen to them because that's just life. So they are not actively engaged in the war, even though they are on the receiving end of the consequences of the war. But God wants us to always remember that "He who is in you is greater than he who is in the world" (1 John 4:4). Keep this in your mind at all times.

Remember, you don't have to be at war with anyone in order for them to be at war with you. But God has given us a way to take dominion over the enemy. It's by praying in Jesus' name, backed up by the Word of God. Jesus suffered and died for us and won power over death and hell. The battle happens as we pray.

We may think once we resist the enemy in prayer the battle is over, and that must mean the *war* is over too. But keep in mind that the war is *never* over. The enemy will always try to draw us into submission to his plans as long as we are here on earth. Remember that *prayer* is the *actual battle*. God taught us to pray, "Do not lead us into temptation, but deliver us from the evil one. For Yours is the kingdom and the power and the glory forever. Amen" (Matthew 6:13). He is saying to pray that you will not be led into temptation by the enemy, but instead you will be delivered from the evil one because God is all-powerful and glorified forever.

Don't be afraid. You can do this. In fact, you can be deployed in God's army without ever having to go anywhere outside of your favorite prayer place in your home. Father God is calling you both to fight powerfully on His side in this war. Will you answer that call?

His Prayer

Lord, we thank You that You are stronger than anything we may face in our lives together. We are grateful we can resist the enemy of our souls, and he will have to flee.

Teach my wife and me to build our lives together on the solid foundation of Your Word. Make us powerful together in prayer so that we cannot be shaken. Thank You that You have made our prayers to be the battle we raise up as the greatest resistance of the enemy's advance in our lives. And nothing can stand against it. Enable us to hear one another's concerns and fulfill Your law by bearing one another's burdens in prayer (see Galatians 6:2).

Help us to always hear Your voice speaking to our hearts about how to pray regarding certain challenges we are facing. Teach us to see that we aren't just asking for things, but that You want us to specifically battle against the works of evil as we pray. We are privileged to be a part of Your great army of prayer warriors who have heard Your call to pray against the evil we see in the world. Teach us to recognize the true spiritual power You have given us by Your victory on the cross. We know that "though we walk in the flesh, we do not war according to the flesh. For the weapons of our warfare are not carnal but mighty in God for pulling down strongholds, casting down arguments and every high thing that exalts itself against the knowledge of God, bringing every thought into captivity to the obedience of Christ" (2 Corinthians 10:3-5). Enable us to always believe the truth of this, Your Word, so we can bring our thoughts into obedience to You. Teach us to clearly hear when You call us to pray against the evil powers of this world that we see advancing daily.

In Jesus' name I pray.

Personal Prayer Needs

_____

_____

Her Prayer

Thank You, Lord God, for teaching us how to face each day with Your Word in our hearts and Your will on our minds. Help us to always be able to identify any work of darkness that is trying to attack either of us or our marriage relationship or our family members. Teach us to always distinguish immediately whose side we are on. We choose to be on *Your* side, but if we are not seeing that the enemy is opposing us, open our eyes to see the truth. Don't allow us to be deceived. You are our true and living God, and we live with Your Word in our heart. The enemy only has power in our lives if we allow him to. Keep us from ever making that mistake.

Thank You, Jesus, that You taught us how to pray, and You lived that example out every day of Your life. Thank You that You have already won this war. Your Word says we do not wrestle against people as much as it is against "the rulers of the darkness of this age, against spiritual hosts of wickedness" (Ephesians 6:12). Enable us to never forget that. Help us to be every day in prayer for our protection and the protection of others so we will always win the battle and defeat the enemy. Teach us to proclaim Your Word every day that says no weapon formed against us by the enemy will prosper (see Isaiah 54:17). Enable us to stand strong in Your love whenever we face an enemy attack against the powerful truth of these words.

In Jesus' name I pray.

Personal Prayer Needs

_____

_____

TRUTH TO AGREE ON

No weapon formed against you shall prosper,
and every tongue which rises against you in judgment
you shall condemn.

ISAIAH 54:17

Blessed be the LORD my Rock,
who trains my hands for war, and my fingers for battle—
my lovingkindness and my fortress,
my high tower and my deliverer,
my shield and the One in whom I take refuge.

PSALM 144:1-2

Submit to God. Resist the devil and he will flee from you.
Draw near to God and He will draw near to you…
Humble yourselves in the sight of the Lord,
and He will lift you up.

JAMES 4:7-8, 10

Let us cast off the works of darkness,
and let us put on the armor of light.

ROMANS 13:12

You will light my lamp; the LORD my God
will enlighten my darkness.
For by You I can run against a troop,
by my God I can leap over a wall.
As for God, His way is perfect; the word of the LORD
is proven; He is a shield to all who trust in Him.

PSALM 18:28-30

CHAPTER 10

Discovering the Power
of Praising God

One of the strongest unifiers between a husband and wife is worship. It will hopefully be easy to agree on *whom* you are praying *to*, and *whom* you worship, and what He promises to you when you invite Him into your heart forever. The truth is, the more you know about God, the more you *want* to worship Him. The more you understand all that Jesus did for you when He died on the cross, the more reasons you have to *praise* Him. And the more you understand about all the Holy Spirit of God enables you to do, the more you will give thanks to your Comforter. That's why it's good to start every prayer with adoration, appreciation, thanks, praise, and worship to God for loving you and hearing your prayers, and all He *has* done, and *is* doing, and *will* do in your life.

What many people don't realize is that power is released in your heart every time you worship God. We all worship something, and whatever we worship will become the main motivator in our lives. *We* choose. We can worship money, possessions, entertainment, and other people, to name a few options. And we will always become like what we worship.

It says in the Bible of those who worship idols, "Those who make them are like them; so is everyone who trusts in them" (Psalm 115:8).

The good news is the more you worship *God*, the more you become like *Him*. The bad news is the more you worship other gods, the more you become like *them*. But they cannot save you or deliver you. Only our *God* of the universe can. They cannot change you or transform you. Only our magnificent and merciful *God* can.

One of the most wonderful things about God is that He shares Himself with us when we worship Him. We grow to understand more of who He really is when we praise Him. The Bible says there "have been given to us exceedingly great and precious promises, that through these *you may be partakers of the divine nature*, having escaped the corruption that is in the world through lust" (2 Peter 1:4). God doesn't need to be reminded of who He is, but *we always* need to be reminded of it. He knows that *we do* need to *show Him* that we recognize and appreciate His greatness, power, and love. God wants our worship of Him to be our greatest blessing as He fulfills us, feeds us, and restores us.

Our praise and worship of God become the very means by which God fills us with His love, peace, and joy. When we worship Him, we take the focus off ourselves and put it entirely on Him. We will never truly know joy until we find it in Him. The Bible says, "Do not sorrow, for the joy of the LORD is your strength" (Nehemiah 8:10). That joy is real, and the strength it brings is clearly perceivable.

Sometimes, *all* God wants from you is to stop and simply worship Him. Lifting up your heart and your hands to the Lord means you have to let go of everything you are hanging on to that is not from Him. (Don't try this when you're driving.) Too often, *we* try to take charge of our lives because we think *we* have to make our lives happen. But God wants us to *let go* of our lives and *hang on* to *Him* so *He* can make our lives happen. We do that every time we lift up our heart to Him in worship.

We were created to worship God. It's where we find the greatest peace and rest. In some situations you may find that your worship together as a couple will be the very thing that changes a situation that seems unchangeable. That's because you are worshipping the God who can change anything and everything. Be specific in what you agree on about God that makes Him worthy of your praise. This is most important when finding oneness and unity between you. Remember, being one doesn't make you into someone you are not; it allows each of you to become who God made you to be. You will complement one another in ways you never thought possible.

Your relationship with God and your relationship with your spouse are the most important relationships you will have in your life. And when they are good, they are life transforming in every way. It will be amazing how much will be accomplished in both of your lives if worship is the first encounter you have with the Lord each day. It puts everything in perspective.

His Prayer

Lord, we worship You as our Lord and Savior, our Healer and Redeemer, our Provider and Strength. We give thanks to You for Your goodness and mercy to us. Continue to fill us with Your love so that we become more like You. Help us to always remember to praise and worship You every day, no matter what is happening in our lives. Thank You that You share Yourself with us as we worship You, and in this way You enable us to become more like You.

You are our all-powerful King of the universe. There is nothing too hard for You. You are the God of the impossible. We know there is no one who has hardened his heart against You and continued to do well. Thank You that Your power helps us to transcend our weakness, and we are eternally grateful for this.

Open our eyes to see if we ever are tempted to worship idols. Teach us to discern the truth when we give allegiance to things that are the work of godless people. They do nothing but separate us from You and keep us from becoming all You made us to be. Thank You for Your love, protection, and unfailing power on our behalf. Thank You for sharing Yourself with us when we lift up worship and praise to You. It is our greatest privilege to be able to honor You every day with heartfelt worship before You.

In Jesus' name I pray.

Personal Prayer Needs

_____

_____

Her Prayer

Lord, we worship You as our all-knowing and all-seeing God of the universe. We praise You because You see our past and our future, and You are with us always. You never leave nor forsake those who love You and praise You with their whole heart. You are all-powerful, and nothing is too hard for You. You are the God of the impossible. Your Word says that *power* belongs to *You* (see Psalm 62:11). Only by believing lies from the enemy can we be made to think otherwise. Keep us from being deceived by the enemy's attempts to convince us that he is more powerful than You. That can never be true. Thank You that You are almighty and all-powerful.

You are the Keeper of our hearts and the Forgiver of our souls. Enable us to rise above our own limitations to see things from Your perspective. Empower us to do great things for Your kingdom. Don't let our own dreams and plans for our future get in the way of what Your plan is for our lives.

Thank You that as we wait on You our strength is renewed, and we will run and not grow weary (see Isaiah 40:29-31). Thank You that You meet all our needs. Thank You that even though we can't always see a solution to our problems, You can. And You are more than powerful enough to make that solution happen. We worship You forever as our God of mercy, grace, and love.

In Jesus' name I pray.

Personal Prayer Needs

_____

_____

TRUTH TO AGREE ON

You are a chosen generation, a royal priesthood, a holy nation,
His own special people, that you may proclaim the praises
of Him who called you out of darkness
into His marvelous light.

1 Peter 2:9

Let us continually offer the sacrifice of praise to God,
that is, the fruit of our lips, giving thanks to His name.

Hebrews 13:15

Rejoice in the Lord always.
Again I will say, rejoice!

Philippians 4:4

The eyes of the Lord run to and fro
throughout the whole earth,
to show Himself strong on behalf of those
whose heart is loyal to Him.

2 Chronicles 16:9

Oh, give thanks to the Lord, for He is good!
For His mercy endures forever.

Psalm 107:1

CHAPTER 11

Deciding to Live God's Way

If we truly love God, we will want to please Him. When we know Him well, our greatest desire will be to obey Him. "This is the love of God, that we keep His commandments. And His commandments are not burdensome" (1 John 5:3). His ways are never impossible because He will help us to live His way when we ask Him to.

Jesus asks you as a married couple to be one, just as He and His Father God are one. This is not about criticizing your spouse into an agreement about everything *you* think. That never works. It's about praying together and asking God to work in both of you a oneness so great that it is like the way Jesus and God are perfectly one.

How do you accomplish that kind of oneness on your own? It doesn't just happen. You have to ask God to work that in both of you. You have to desire it and believe God can work His will in you because He can do anything in you that you are open to. He is even able to align your will with His. The Bible says, "Do not be unwise, but understand what the will of the Lord is" (Ephesians 5:17). You need to ask often what God's will is for your lives, and not assume you know. The Bible says, "'My thoughts are not your thoughts, nor are your ways My ways,' says the LORD. 'For as the heavens are higher than the earth, so are My ways higher than your ways, and My thoughts than your thoughts'" (Isaiah 55:8-9). We must respect His ways and be humble enough to not think we know everything. Or that we know more than God about what's best for us. We must remember that His ways and thoughts are much greater than ours, so we need to ask Him to help us understand His ways. He wants that from us.

When you have a heart for God, you will also develop a love for His Word. That's where His will and ways are revealed. You will see that as you walk in His ways your greatest blessings happen for you. That's why His ways become very important things to agree on and pray about.

You can always learn to walk *closer* with God and know Him *better*. So it's best if you and your spouse can stay on the same level of desire to know Him. But that doesn't mean if your husband or wife is not the least bit interested in growing into a deeper relationship with God that you should slow down *your* relationship with Him. Don't step back in your walk with God to become so disinterested in it as to match the attitude of your husband or wife. Just be kind and patient with your spouse about it, and keep praying together more. Or read the Bible together, or go to a church together that you both feel at home in. We are not always in the same place at the same time, but that doesn't mean you won't ever be, or can't be, or never will be. It means that you both have to give mercy and grace to the other whenever it's needed as God grows you together. The problem with us is that we often want to do what *we* want more than we want to do what *God* wants. We can even become selfish and think only of ourselves instead of constantly filling our heart with God's truth about His ways. That takes being in prayer and in His Word.

You must make a choice each day—hopefully together—that you *want* to live God's way. That's what this chapter is about.

Praying together to ask God to write His ways on Your heart. The Bible says, "Where there is no revelation, the people cast off restraint; but happy is he who keeps the law" (Proverbs 29:18). It also says, "Great peace have those who love Your law, and nothing causes them to stumble" (Psalm 119:165). Peace and safety are your reward for living God's way. Keep in mind that even when *you* can't see a way, *God* can.

His Prayer

Lord, thank You for loving us enough to want us to agree together on how much *we* love *You* and desire to serve You by living Your way. We are grateful for Your precepts because we know that living according to Your laws brings our greatest blessings. Give each of us a heart that longs to know You better. Teach us Your ways and help us to love and obey them. Help us to want Your ways more than our own selfish desires. When we are in doubt about what Your laws are, enable us to discern them clearly in Your Word.

Reveal to us any area of our lives where we are not living in obedience to You. Keep us from drifting away from the things we have already learned about You, and from ever thinking we have learned so much from Your Word that we don't need to be as diligent about that anymore. We know that we cannot assume we will never be tempted to move away from what we have learned about You because the enemy of our souls and our marriage is always wanting to destroy both.

We know from Your Word that Your ways and thoughts are higher than ours, and we have the utmost respect for them and You. We want to choose every day to follow You. Bring Your Word alive in our hearts and minds every time we read it—whether alone or together. Give us such a love for Your law and ways that it keeps us from ever stumbling.

In Jesus' name I pray.

Personal Prayer Needs

_____

_____

Her Prayer

Lord, we thank You for Your laws and ways. We know they are good and that You have established them for our benefit. Open our eyes to see if there are any places in us where we are not obeying them in our lives. Enable us to always live in obedience to Your precepts. Keep us from ever straying from what we have learned so we don't start walking in disobedience to any of Your commandments.

Keep us undeceived so we never think that we are incapable of sin because Your Word says, "If we say that we have no sin, we deceive ourselves, and the truth is not in us" (1 John 1:8). Enable us to see immediately if either of us has fallen into deception. Help us to choose each day to stand strong together and live *Your* way. Keep us from relying on our own understanding, but instead help us to determine every day to rely on *Your truth*.

We know that You want us to walk ever closer to You because You want the best for us. Keep us in full agreement that Your ways work in our lives, and when we don't live Your way, life doesn't work. Help each of us to be patient, merciful, and full of grace with each other, just as You are with each of us. Grow us continually together and strong enough to choose each day that we will live Your way, and follow Your leading as we pray to understand what that is.

In Jesus' name I pray.

Personal Prayer Needs

_____

_____

TRUTH TO AGREE ON

Whoever keeps His word,
truly the love of God is perfected in him.
By this we know that we are in Him.

1 JOHN 2:5

You shall observe My statutes
and keep My judgments, and perform them;
and you will dwell in the land in safety.

LEVITICUS 25:18

Behold, I set before you today a blessing and a curse:
the blessing, if you obey the commandments
of the LORD your God which I command you today.

DEUTERONOMY 11:26-27

Blessed are those who hear
the word of God and keep it!

LUKE 11:28

If I regard iniquity in my heart,
the LORD will not hear.

PSALM 66:18

CHAPTER 12

Growing Together in Faith

Many say that life really begins with our faith in God. Everything that is most important in life is ignited within us when we have true faith. The Bible says, "God has dealt to each one a measure of faith" (Romans 12:3). Otherwise, how could we be saved through faith (see Ephesians 2:8)? Faith starts as a gift from God in the beginning. But having strong faith is an ongoing growth process. We need to be ever-increasing in faith—and especially when it comes to our marriage.

It's possible to have faith in God to do great things in your marriage relationship. And that happens as you allow Him to change you to be more like *Him*. Remember the promise in Matthew 18:20 that where two or more are gathered in the name of Jesus, God's presence is there in the midst of them? That means the greatest changes in the two of you as a couple will happen when you pray together.

For example, at some point it may seem impossible to you that you and your husband or wife could live in unity. But that is not the case when you both have strong faith in the God of the impossible. The Bible says, "Without faith it is impossible to please Him, for he who comes to God must believe that He is, and that He is a rewarder of those who diligently seek Him" (Hebrews 11:6). This is a great "Truth to Agree On." Start with believing God exists and that He rewards you when you pray and seek Him for everything. The Bible says, "Whatever is not from faith is sin" (Romans 14:23). That makes it very clear how necessary it is to believe what God says in His Word. Your prayers together about this should be that God will help you both keep growing in faith.

No matter what your faith is like now, if you need a miracle in your marriage or in your lives, God can increase your faith for that. That doesn't mean you always get whatever you ask for at that moment. You have to have faith that God hears your prayers, and that He will answer in His way and in His timing. This is very important. Your faith is in *Him* and not in *how* or *whether* He answers the way you want Him to.

The Bible says, "According to your faith let it be to you" (Matthew 9:29). That can be a scary thought if your faith is weak. The Bible says of someone who is full of doubt about the power of God to do miracles for us, "Let him ask in faith, *with no doubting,* for he who doubts is like a wave of the sea driven and tossed by the wind. For let not that man suppose that he will receive anything from the Lord; he is a double-minded man, unstable in all his ways" (James 1:6-8). Anyone who is weak in faith will get nothing from God. You don't want that.

Keep reading the Word—together and alone whenever you can—and decide what promise of God you both would like to claim as your own each day. Think of it as if God has spoken it to you specifically—because He has. The Bible says, "Faith comes by hearing, and hearing by the word of God" (Romans 10:17). Keep reading and listening.

Don't worry if your spouse hesitates to pray with you or has little faith. You can still pray alone or with a prayer partner about this. Just make certain the prayer partner is one you can trust to keep your prayer requests for your husband or wife private. You do not need a prayer partner who has loose lips and acts as the town crier, sharing people's private requests. That will never work and can turn off your husband or wife to trusting any "believers."

When Jesus was here on earth, a woman who had a flow of blood for 12 years tried to get close to Him in a crowd. As He walked by her, she said to herself, "'If only I may touch His garment, I shall be made well.' But Jesus turned around, and when He saw her, He said, 'Be of good cheer, daughter; *your faith has made you well.* And the woman was made well from that hour" (Matthew 9:20-22). Whenever you reach out to God in prayer and touch Him in faith, your lives will be healed in some way. Remember this whenever you start to have doubt about God's ability to hear and answer your prayers.

His Prayer

Thank You, Lord, that You teach us to "walk by faith, not by sight," as You have said in Your Word (2 Corinthians 5:7). I pray that You would enable my wife and me to have strong faith so we can pray and stand strong in faith together to believe for the healing, restoration, transformation, provision—or whatever else we need to see happen—for ourselves and others for whom we pray. Thank You that You are able to keep us from falling into doubt and lose our way.

Teach us how to take the "shield of faith," to "quench all the fiery darts of the wicked one" whenever we feel attacked by the enemy (Ephesians 6:16). Enable us to clearly see our faith as a shield of protection. Keep us from becoming doubters who are tossed around like a wave of the sea so that we are unstable and unable to receive all You have for us. We cannot bear it if our lack of faith does not please You, and as a result would cause us to not move into all You have for us. We believe in You as our Lord and Savior, Healer and Deliverer. And we know when we come to You in faith, You reward us. Grow us together in our faith in You and Your Word. Help us to always believe Your Word that says, "All things are possible to him who believes" (Mark 9:23). Help us to keep that truth in the forefront of our minds as we pray together in unity of purpose.

In Jesus' name I pray.

Personal Prayer Needs

_____

_____

Her Prayer

Lord, You say in Your Word that if we have faith, nothing will be impossible for us (see Matthew 17:20). We know our faith is in You and not our ability to have faith. So teach my husband and me to have strong faith in You that is always increasing. Keep both of us consistently in Your Word because You have said that we increase in faith when we read it or hear it. You have given us some faith in order to believe in You and receive You as our Lord and Savior. Your Word says You have given each of us "a measure of faith" (see Romans 12:3). Increase our faith every day.

Regarding our marriage and our lives together, enable each of us to steadily grow in faith so that we can stand strong and believe for a miracle from You when we pray for one. You can resurrect anything in us, and that keeps us from giving up on each other whenever we have a problem or misunderstanding. Lord, teach us to "let patience have its perfect work" in us, that we may be "perfect and complete, lacking nothing" (James 1:4).

We don't want to sin against You by giving place to our doubts. For Your Word says that "whatever is not from faith is sin" (Romans 14:23). Keep us from all sin, but especially the sin of doubt. Remind us clearly to repent before You whenever we allow ourselves to doubt Your Word and what we know You have spoken to our heart.

In Jesus' name I pray.

Personal Prayer Needs

_____

_____

TRUTH TO AGREE ON

We walk by faith, not by sight.

2 CORINTHIANS 5:7

Faith is the substance of things hoped for,
the evidence of things not seen.

HEBREWS 11:1

If you have faith as a mustard seed, you will say to this mountain,
"Move from here to there," and it will move;
and nothing will be impossible for you.

MATTHEW 17:20

In this you greatly rejoice, though now for a little while,
if need be, you have been grieved by various trials,
that the genuineness of your faith, being much more precious
than gold that perishes, though it is tested by fire,
may be found to praise, honor, and glory
at the revelation of Jesus Christ.

1 PETER 1:6-7

Your faith should not be in the wisdom of men
but in the power of God.

1 CORINTHIANS 2:5

CHAPTER 13

Respecting God's Gift of Health

I f either of you struggle with taking good care of your body, you can ask God to help you live the right way to maintain it. Whether it's because you don't know *what* to change or *how* to change what you have been doing—or if you *do* know what you are doing wrong but don't feel you have the will or power to make the change needed—God will show you and enable you to do what's right for you. The good news is *God is always on your side*, and He is willing to reveal to you whatever is necessary to keep you whole as far as it is up to you. And He will give you the strength and power to do what is necessary.

It doesn't have to be an overwhelming task. The way God wants you to live is doable and a definite act of obedience God wants from you. Remember, His ways are for your benefit. Always!

People who severely abuse their bodies with drugs, alcohol, smoking, bad or unhealthy food, and many other things don't always consider what this does to their family and friends who care about them. For the spouse of the person who is careless about his or her health, it seems as though their husband or wife doesn't love them enough to do whatever they can to stay alive and present for them and their children. God cares about that as well—even more than you do. The Bible says, "Do you not know that you are the temple of God and that the Spirit of God dwells in you? If anyone defiles the temple of God, God will destroy him. For the temple of God is holy, which temple you are" (1 Corinthians 3:16-17). God is serious about this. How we treat our body is important to Him because His Spirit dwells within us. It should be as important to you as well. It definitely is to your husband or wife. If we are intent on destroying our body, which is the temple of God, He may just let you do what you are intent on doing. Whether or not you think of it as destroying yourself, you are the temple of the Holy Spirit, and you have to start seeing that from God's perspective.

It's very upsetting to see your spouse doing things to shorten his or her life. And it's not only what you eat or drink that does not sustain life or health. It could be burning the candle at both ends so you have too little rest and too much stress. This is something you must agree on in prayer. These things can change. It's not too late. Ask yourself and each other, "Are you taking care of God's temple to the best of your ability?" Ask God to show you. There may be things you need to see that He wants to reveal to you.

Value the body God gave you. If there are things that need to be repaired in your body, get them taken care of. Ask God to help you find the right people who know what needs to be done. Don't ignore health warnings when you see them. Your believing loved ones will thank you and help you pray through anything you are going through. Sometimes our health is not a matter of what we eat or how much we exercise. It's how we think. For example, the Bible says, "A sound heart is life to the body, but envy is rottenness to the bones" (Proverbs 14:30). Ongoing negative attitudes such as envy or unforgiveness can damage our health far more than certain foods can.

Think of it as your ministry to the Lord. The Bible says,

"Whatever you eat or drink, or whatever you do, do all to the glory of God" (1 Corinthians 10:31). In other words, think of the way you treat your body as a way to glorify and please God. Taking care of yourself is a way to bless Him because it's one of the ways you serve Him.

Sometimes, though, through no fault of your own—or at least not to your knowledge—you will need God's healing. The good news is Jesus came as your healer because He knew you would need it. So don't hesitate to ask God for healing. He is referred to as "the Lord who heals you" (Exodus 15:26). There is nothing more precious than our salvation, but He also loves us enough to provide for our healing. What greater love than this is there?

His Prayer

Lord, thank You that You care about our health. Thank You that You will reveal to us anything we need to *start* doing—or *stop* doing—that will give us better health. Thank You also that You are our healer. You knew we needed a healer, and You paid the price so we can turn to You in faith, and You hear our prayers for healing—in Your way and time.

I pray that both my wife and I will be open to hear from You about the way we respect the gift of health and life You have given us. We want to glorify You in the way we value the body we have and not do anything to minimize our health in any way.

Help us to understand that our bodies are Your temple and that we need to take care of them as part of our obedience to You and as another way to glorify You. Open our eyes to do this before any careless ways we already have may cause us to destroy our health. Give us wisdom to do the right things. Lead us to knowledgeable professional people to help us when we need guidance. Give us clear discernment to know what is good for us and what isn't. Give us both strength and unity of resolve to do the right thing.

Teach us to not focus on what we disagree on, but what we *do* agree on. We agree that we want to please You, Lord. We agree that You are our healer. Help us to extend mercy and grace to one another as we work through these things together. We trust You to teach us the right things to do or not do.

Above all, we are thankful that You are the Lord who heals us. Give us strong faith to pray and have faith for that.

In Jesus' name I pray.

Personal Prayer Needs

_____

_____

Her Prayer

Lord, we trust You and need You to help us live long and healthy lives. Thank You for Your guidance to help us learn to live right. Teach us to remember that our bodies are the temple of Your Holy Spirit who dwells in us, and we have been bought at a price and are not our own (see 1 Corinthians 6:19-20). Etch that in our minds and hearts and cause us to be in unity about this so that we will always try to do the right things. Teach us how to make excellent choices regarding how we take care of our bodies. Enable us to reject anything that either of us is doing that undermines our good health. Give us an openness with each other to share where we have concerns about ourselves or each other. Open our eyes to see any place where we have careless or clueless health care habits that will ultimately be life destroying. Teach us what to avoid and what to include. Help us to be good stewards of our bodies and never take the health we have for granted.

Your Word says, "Your ears shall hear a word behind you, saying, 'This is the way, walk in it,' whenever you turn to the right hand or whenever you turn to the left" (Isaiah 30:21). Enable us to always hear Your voice speaking to us about the way we should go in every part of our life. We want to always serve You, please You, and glorify You, especially in the way we treat our bodies. Thank You that You are our healer who came to heal us. Give us strong faith to believe for Your healing touch in our lives.

In Jesus' name I pray.

Personal Prayer Needs

_____

_____

TRUTH TO AGREE ON

I beseech you therefore, brethren, by the mercies of God,
that you present your bodies a living sacrifice,
holy, acceptable to God, which is your reasonable service.

ROMANS 12:1

Do you not know that your body
is the temple of the Holy Spirit who is in you,
whom you have from God, and you are not your own?
For you were bought at a price; therefore glorify God
in your body and in your spirit, which are God's.

1 CORINTHIANS 6:19-20

If you diligently heed the voice of the LORD your God
and do what is right in His sight,
give ear to His commandments and keep all His statutes,
I will put none of the diseases on you
which I have brought on the Egyptians.
For I am the LORD who heals you.

EXODUS 15:26

The prayer of faith will save the sick,
and the LORD will raise him up.

JAMES 5:15

"I will restore health to you
and heal you of your wounds," says the LORD.

JEREMIAH 30:17

CHAPTER 14

Producing the Fruit of the Spirit

Every day we plant seeds in our lives. Each choice we make can plant a good seed or a bad seed. *We* choose. God's Word asks us to "put on tender mercies, kindness, humility, meekness, long-suffering" (Colossians 3:12). We *specifically* put on these things as a choice we make. As a seed we plant. We choose these characteristics to be a part of who we are. We could just wait to see what grows up in our lives and either be pleased or disappointed in what the future holds. Or we can ask God to help us plant good seeds every day so we can produce the fruit of His Spirit and not the weeds of our flesh. He is more than pleased to help us do that.

Our lives now are a result of what we have planted in the past. We reap the good and the bad for quite a while after we have sown the seeds. In fact, today we may still be reaping some of the fruit of the flesh we have planted in the past. But we can also choose to plant the seeds of the Spirit right now. Jesus said that He is the vine and you and your husband or wife are the branches (see John 15:5). If you live in His way every day, you will always bear good fruit—that is, the fruit of His Spirit.

The Bible says, "The fruit of the Spirit is love, joy, peace, longsuffering, kindness, goodness, faithfulness, gentleness, self-control. Against such there is no law" (Galatians 5:22-23). It's very clear what kind of crop we are to produce. That's why it's good for each of you to pray, "Lord, cause the fruit of Your Spirit to be manifested in me." It's certain that when you invite the life of God's Spirit to live in you, and you live your life in Him, that is what will happen.

Always keep in mind that you are planting something every day in your life, and especially in your marriage relationship. The seeds you plant will always take root and grow. If you plant seeds of bitterness, rudeness, resentment, discord, negativity, criticism, and lovelessness—the fruit of the flesh—you will reap a full-grown version of those things in your lives and in your relationship. Who wants to live in a miserable marriage? No one. But if you practice planting seeds of love, peace, and joy; patience, kindness, and goodness; faithfulness, gentleness, and self-control—the fruit of the Spirit—that is what you will find growing in your marriage, and the result will be beautiful.

Producing the fruit of the Spirit in your life makes you a compelling, attractive, and desirable person. Everyone wants to be around that person. Having a facial expression that is always negative—the exact opposite of the fruit-of-the-Spirit face—causes people to run the other way. The good news is that these nine words represent the character of God. So stick close to Him in prayer, and these seeds will produce a great crop of spiritual fruit in you that you won't want to live without.

In order to always plant good seeds that will produce the fruit of the Spirit in your lives, you must make a decision to not walk in the flesh. Our flesh is weak, but God's Spirit in us is strong. We have to stay strong. We have to stay close to God. The Bible says, "Each one is tempted when he is *drawn away* by his *own desires* and enticed" (James 1:14). So if you start to have a thought that is born of the flesh—a thought of temptation toward a fleshly action—confess it to God and lift up praise and worship to Him. Thank Him for His greatness and goodness to rule over this situation. Praise Him that He is more powerful than anything you might face in the way of temptation.

Whatever you do, don't avoid God because of things in your mind or life that should not be there. Your praise and worship will break through all that. You may feel unworthy to be forgiven of the sins of the flesh. But the quicker you come before God in humility, confession, and worship, the quicker you can be cleansed of sin—or avoid the consequences of it altogether.

Everyone makes mistakes. So don't let your guilt over anything keep you from coming before God. Seek His presence and ask Him to rule in your life so you will always produce good fruit.

His Prayer

Lord, thank You that You give us the fruit of Your Spirit when we plant good seeds from Your Word in our lives together. Thank You that You help us to move in the Spirit when we worship You and live according to Your ways.

I pray You would plant the fruit of Your Spirit in my wife and me so that we can produce a beautiful crop of the fruit that comes only from You and not from our flesh. Your Word tells us to "let the peace of God our Spirit rule in your hearts" (Colossians 3:15), and "by your patience possess your souls" (Luke 21:19). We ask for that in every area of our lives. Only with Your help can we produce any of the fruit of Your Spirit that You have for us.

You have said that if we abide in You and Your words abide in us, we can ask what we desire, and it will be done for us (see John 15:7). We desire that You will plant us by the rivers of Your living water, so that we can bring forth fruit in season that won't wither (see Psalm 1:3). Help us to stay on the path close to You—our true vine—so that we never stray away from Your living water. Without You we can do nothing.

I pray that we will live and walk with You, and Your Words and truth will live in our hearts and minds, so that when we ask of You what we desire, You will hear our prayer and answer.

In Jesus' name I pray.

Personal Prayer Needs

_____

_____

Her Prayer

Lord, we praise You for the fruit of Your Spirit, which is "love, joy, peace, longsuffering, kindness, goodness, faithfulness, gentleness, self-control" (Galatians 5:22-23). We know that only as we live in You, and let Your Spirit rule in us, can we produce that kind of godly fruit in our lives. Help us to refuse to give place to traits of our flesh, especially toward one another. Rather help us to show these attitudes of mind and heart toward each other so that it causes us to produce life and not death in our relationship.

We know from Your Word that when we bear good fruit, You are glorified. Help us to glorify You in that way every day. Teach us to plant the right seeds in our hearts so we can produce the life You want for us. Enable us to dwell with You and welcome You to dwell with us every day, so that we will always bear the fruit of Your Spirit and not our flesh. Cause us to fully repent before You and each other if we slip into sinful fleshly attitudes.

I pray Your *love* will flow through us to each other, and Your *joy* will rise up in our hearts so Your *peace* in us will bring peace to each other as well as those around us. By our *patience* help us to be perfected, and by our *kindness* and *goodness* let us see You in each other. By our faithfulness, gentleness, and self-control, may others see You in us and in our marriage. We desire that each of the fruits of Your Spirit will be seen clearly in both of us so that we may become all You created us to be.

In Jesus' name I pray.

Personal Prayer Needs

_____

_____

TRUTH TO AGREE ON

I am the true vine, and My Father is the vinedresser.
Every branch in Me that does not bear fruit He takes away;
and every branch that bears fruit He prunes,
that it may bear more fruit.

JOHN 15:1-2

Abide in Me, and I in you.
As the branch cannot bear fruit of itself,
unless it abides in the vine,
neither can you, unless you abide in Me.

JOHN 15:4

I am the vine, you are the branches.
He who abides in Me, and I in him, bears much fruit;
for without Me you can do nothing.

JOHN 15:5

If you abide in Me, and My words abide in you,
you will ask what you desire, and it shall be done for you.
By this My Father is glorified, that you bear much fruit;
so you will be My disciples.

JOHN 15:7-8

If you keep My commandments, you will abide in My love,
just as I have kept My Father's commandments
and abide in His love.

JOHN 15:10

CHAPTER 15

Seeking God's Kingdom First

When John the Baptist was preparing people to receive the ministry of Jesus, he went about saying, "Repent, for the kingdom of heaven is at hand!" (Matthew 3:2). He was talking about King Jesus, who had come to destroy the forces of hell. The kingdom of heaven was near because the King was there.

Jesus said that the kingdom of God is a spiritual kingdom and not a worldly kingdom. It comes from God, and Jesus is the King. He said in Luke 17:21 that the kingdom of God exists wherever believers in Jesus invite Him to rule in their heart and life.

In order to seek God's kingdom, we must be teachable, free of all arrogance, and humble. Jesus said, "Blessed are the poor in spirit, for theirs is the kingdom of heaven" (Matthew 5:3). The poor in spirit have the distinct advantage of not thinking they know everything. They are teachable regarding the things of God.

The Bible says, "Every good gift and every perfect gift is from above, and comes down from the Father of lights, with whom there is no variation or shadow of turning" (James 1:17). God is the source of good and not evil, and He doesn't change. But in order to receive the good things He has for you, you must *first seek God* and His kingdom. God wants us to seek Him for everything He has for us.

We may not even know that we are doing it, but often we think we can handle our own life in our own way, and we'll call on God if we need Him. He does not want us to make that assumption. God says that is prideful on our part, and He wants us to recognize that we need Him for everything because everything we need comes from Him. Only when we *know* how much we *need* the *Lord* can we truly experience the kingdom of God.

Basically, what we seek is Him. One of the things we seek in Him is His power working in us. The Bible says, "Eye has not seen, nor ear heard, nor have entered into the heart of man the things which God has prepared for those who love Him" (1 Corinthians 2:9). Isn't that a great promise? But it all starts with seeking Him first, above all else. And declaring your dependance upon Him.

Jesus said, "It is easier for a camel to go through the eye of a needle than for a rich man to enter the kingdom of God" (Matthew 19:24). That means it's impossible to trust anything in the world to get you into the kingdom of God. You have to receive King Jesus first in order to have the way to receive the kingdom of God. So we must come humbly before Him declaring that we cannot live without Him.

When you lift up praise to God before you do anything else, you are lifted above all doubt, fleshly concerns, discontent, and selfishness, thereby allowing yourself to be swept up by the things of God to where you cannot make mistakes. Away from faithlessness and into faith. Away from a bad spirit and into having a right spirit within you.

The Bible says, "Those who live according to the flesh set their minds on the things of the flesh, but those who live according to the Spirit, the things of the Spirit. For to be carnally minded is death, but to be spiritually minded is life and peace" (Romans 8:5-6).

After the part in the Bible where Jesus talked about seeking

God's kingdom, the next thing He says is, "Do not fear, little flock, for it is Your Father's good pleasure to give you the king-dom" (Luke 12:32). He knows what you need, and He wants you to look to Him for that (see Matthew 6:32).

His Prayer

Lord, thank You that when we seek You first in all things, You reign in our hearts, and we have whatever we need. Thank You for giving good gifts to Your children who love You and seek You with all of our heart. I pray that my wife and I will learn to seek You first in all things. We want You to be the first one we turn to each day to invite Your kingdom to fill our hearts afresh. Help us to remember that every good gift comes from You, and that Your kingdom is within us. We don't need to look anywhere else to find what we need. It can all be found in You when we seek You.

We don't ever want to think we *know* everything, and that we can *do* all things on our own. Keep us from ever thinking pridefully. Your Word says that we don't inherit Your kingdom by any accomplishment in our flesh. Jesus said clearly, "Most assuredly, I say to you, unless one is born again, he cannot see the kingdom of God" (John 3:3). You never said to us, "Don't pray about it." You said to seek Your kingdom and righteousness first, and You will supply all our needs (see Matthew 6:33). Thank You, Lord, that You love us so much that when we seek You first, we don't have to worry about everything because You have it all in Your hands.

In Jesus' name I pray.

Personal Prayer Needs

_____

_____

Her Prayer

Thank You, Lord, that You have said, "The kingdom of God is *within* you" (Luke 17:21). It comes *from You*. In order to receive *Your kingdom*, we must *receive You*. Thank You that there are many gifts in Your kingdom which You share with us when we seek You and Your kingdom above all else. We are grateful that whenever we seek You first above all else, and lift up praise to You and exalt You above all things, everything we need will be added to us. Your Word says we have received Your Spirit, so we know what we have been given by You (see 1 Corinthians 2:12).

Lord, help us to keep our priorities clear by seeking Your kingdom first each day. We know that without You we can do nothing. Keep us from trying to accomplish things on our own without first praying to You about everything. Your kingdom is where You, the King of the universe, dwells.

Your Word says that nothing can separate us from Your love and grace, "which is in Christ Jesus our Lord" (Romans 8:39). Because of what You accomplished on the cross, we receive Your love and Your grace without which our life does not work, nor can our marriage. When Your grace is extended to us, it means we don't have to suffer what we deserve. You have already paid that price. Your love is extended to us in our greatest gift. Thank You that You are a good God who gives good things to those who seek You first.

In Jesus' name I pray.

Personal Prayer Needs

_____

_____

TRUTH TO AGREE ON

Seek the kingdom of God,
and all these things shall be added to you.
Do not fear, little flock, for it is your Father's
good pleasure to give you the kingdom.

LUKE 12:31-32

Do not worry, saying, "What shall we eat?" or
"What shall we drink?" or "What shall we wear?"
For after all these things the Gentiles seek.
For your heavenly Father knows that you need all these things.
But seek first the kingdom of God and His righteousness,
and all these things shall be added to you.

MATTHEW 6:31-33

If you then, being evil, know how to give good gifts
to your children, how much more will your Father
who is in heaven give good things to those who ask Him!

MATTHEW 7:11

We have received, not the spirit of the world,
but the Spirit who is from God,
that we might know the things
that have been freely given to us by God.

1 CORINTHIANS 2:12

Flesh and blood cannot inherit the kingdom of God;
nor does corruption inherit incorruption.

1 CORINTHIANS 15:50

CHAPTER 16

Exposing All Pride

Being humble is extremely important—especially before God and in a marriage. The Bible says, "God *resists* the proud, but gives *grace* to the humble" (James 4:6). We do not want God to resist us. In a marriage, arrogance and pride in one person can kill the spirit of the other. Mercy and grace are more in line with the character of Christ. So it's beneficial to grumble less and be grateful more.

Much is said in the Word of God about the negative consequences of pride. Pride is a trap we never want to fall into. People who become prideful don't realize that their true need is for more of the Lord in their hearts and lives. And until they understand that, they are in danger of experiencing a serious fall.

There are *many* young people who do not sense any great lack in their lives because they have always had so much automatically provided for them. We must pray for them—as well as ourselves—to never think that we don't need God for anything. The truth is, we can't accomplish anything good and lasting without God. That's why He wants us to depend on Him for our every need. When we don't recognize our greatest need is for more of Him, things can happen that make us very aware of how much we need Him. It's too easy to fall into *prideful attitudes*, so we have to be *prayerfully watchful* about that. The consequences for not being diligent about it are too great for us to take a chance.

The Bible says to "keep your heart with all diligence, for out of it spring the issues of life" (Proverbs 4:23). We must make a deliberate effort to keep a watchful eye on what is happening in our hearts. The godless world can easily suck us into its spirit. So we have to "watch, stand fast in the faith, be brave, be strong" (1 Corinthians 16:13). The Bible also says, "A man's pride will bring him low, but the humble in spirit will retain honor" (Proverbs 29:23). It is said of God, "Surely He scorns the scornful, but gives grace to the humble" (Proverbs 3:34).

When we live close to God, He helps us to see with our *spiritual* eyes. That's because we who know and love Him have the *mind* of *Christ*. "Where there are envy, strife, and divisions among you, are you not carnal and behaving like mere men?" (1 Corinthians 3:3). Knowing you have the mind of Christ is something you will want to agree on because it will definitely keep you from pride. Knowing you are *in the will of God* is also something to be in agreement about. When you pray about that together, it is powerful. Every person who is humble before God wants that. Only the arrogant want what they want and don't seek the *mind* of *Christ* and the *will* of *God*.

If we do not seek the presence of God in our lives every day, it's easy to get out from under the covering of God's protection, where bad things can happen to us. We can even grow numb to the voice of God speaking to our heart when we listen to the voice of our own pride telling us how we don't need God.

When we depend totally on God—and have been convinced that living without Him did not work as well in the past as we thought it would—then we come to a place of freedom and safety because we see we must depend on Him for everything. We don't live in the pride of our arrogance, which we once for a moment thought was the best place to be. It's not worth it. Better to ask God to keep us from all arrogance and pride, and reveal to us anytime we get close to the edge. Because we don't often see our own pride, it's beneficial to ask God to periodically show us if we have any. Trust me, He will. Without hesitation.

His Prayer

Lord, we know You do not like pride, so we want to quickly confess it before You when we see it in ourselves. But if we don't see it, we lift up our heart to You and ask that You would keep us from being so filled with ourselves that we think we can live without You in any way. Keep us always aware that our greatest need is for more of You. Your Word says that when we say or think that we have no need for You because we think we have everything, what we really are is miserable, poor, blind, and naked (see Revelation 3:17). We don't ever want to be that way.

Your Word says, "You have heard the desire of the humble; You will prepare their heart; You will cause Your ear to hear" (Psalm 10:17). We want to hear everything You speak to our hearts and never miss it. We want You to hear our prayers to You. Keep each of us far from any kind of arrogance with each other. We depend on You for everything, and our greatest need is for more of You in our lives. You are the answer to our every need. We choose to love You more every day and the things of this world less. Let us be known by our love for each other, and also because we love You and keep Your commandments (see 1 John 5:2).

In Jesus' name I pray.

Personal Prayer Needs

_____

_____

Her Prayer

Lord, we come humbly before You, knowing You bless the humble and not the prideful. Show us if there is any pride in my husband or me that needs to be brought before You. We know the terrible arrogance that shows up when we are not aware of our great need for more of You in our lives. Help us to never believe we know everything so that we become unteachable concerning Your ways and Your truth.

Your Word says, "Knowledge puffs up, but love edifies" (1 Corinthians 8:1). It also says, "Everyone who exalts himself will be humbled, and he who humbles himself will be exalted" (Luke 18:14). Keep us from ever becoming puffed up because we think we know better or more than You. Help us to never exalt ourselves, but rather humble ourselves before You and before each other, and exalt You. Enable us to cleanse our hands and purify our hearts so we don't become double-minded (see James 4:8).

Help us to stay in Your Word because it "is living and powerful, and sharper than any two-edged sword, piercing even to the division of soul and spirit, and of joints and marrow, and is a *discerner* of the *thoughts* and *intents* of the heart" (Hebrews 4:12). Give us the ability to immediately discern the thoughts and intents of our hearts if they do not line up with Yours. Expose pride in us, and we will confess it as sin. Take it far away from us. Help us to agree on this principle so we can become all You have made us to be.

In Jesus' name I pray.

Personal Prayer Needs

_____

_____

TRUTH TO AGREE ON

Do not love the world or the things in the world.
If anyone loves the world, the love of the Father
is not in him. For all that is in the world—
the lust of the flesh, the lust of the eyes,
and the pride of life—is not of the Father but is of the world.
And the world is passing away, and the lust of it;
but he who does the will of God abides forever.

1 John 2:15-17

Humble yourselves under the mighty hand of God,
that He may exalt you in due time,
casting all your care upon Him,
for He cares for you.

1 Peter 5:6-7

God resists the proud, but gives grace to the humble.

James 4:6

Thus says the High and Lofty One
who inhabits eternity, whose name is Holy:
"I dwell in the high and holy place,
with him who has a contrite and humble spirit."

Isaiah 57:15

By this we know that we love the children of God,
when we love God and keep His commandments.

1 John 5:2

CHAPTER 17

Standing Ready for the Battle

One of the things we must learn to always do is stand strong in everything we know of God. In order to do that, we have to learn as much about Jesus as we can. We do that by *reading* about Him in His Word and by *spending time* with Him in *prayer* and *worship*. You two as a couple must agree that you are in a never-ending battle with the enemy of your souls—and your marriage. The enemy doesn't like either one, and he will always want to destroy you.

It's clear in God's Word who His enemy is, and *His* enemy is *our* enemy as well. The Bible says, "Though we walk in the flesh, we do not war according to the flesh" (2 Corinthians 10:3). It also says, "We do not wrestle against flesh and blood, but against principalities, against powers, against the rulers of the darkness of this age, against spiritual hosts of wickedness in the heavenly places" (Ephesians 6:12).

We cannot think that after we have fought a battle in prayer that the battle is finished and the war is over. The war is never over. You don't wake up one morning and find that the enemy of your souls—and your marriage—is having a good day and is thinking kind thoughts toward you. That never happens. Of course, we continually have the Lord with us. Jesus said, "I am with you always, even to the end of the age" (Matthew 28:20). In the battle for our marriage, our health, our finances, our work, and our character, God is with us if we invite Him to be. Always ask Him to be on the battlefield with you, remembering the battle is not between you and your spouse. It's a battle between you and the enemy of your soul, marriage, and life—who is also *God's* enemy.

The good news is God has given you spiritual armor to protect you from the enemy of your soul. Putting on the whole armor of God is not something you do when you feel like it. It is something God commanded us all to do every day. If we could withstand evil without doing that, God would have told us. The Bible says, "Take up the whole armor of God, that you may be able to withstand in the evil day, and having done all, to stand" (Ephesians 6:13). Also, "Be strong in the Lord and in the power of His might. Put on the whole armor of God, that you may be able to stand against the wiles of the devil" (Ephesians 6:10-11).

To "stand against" means to oppose the forces and plans of evil. We will *remain standing* before, during, and after the battle if we do that. We are not battling against people, but a spiritual hierarchy of invisible evil power.

Learn to identify the spiritual armor God has given you in Ephesian 6:14-18:

- Stand therefore, having *girded your waist with truth*
  (Read God's truth—the Bible.)

- Having *put on the breastplate of righteousness*
  (You can do the right thing because of the righteousness of Jesus in you.)

- And having *shod your feet with the preparation of the gospel of peace*
  (Know what the Word says about spiritual warfare.)

- Above all, *taking the shield of faith* with which you will be able to quench all the fiery darts of the wicked one (Have faith in God and His almighty power on your behalf.)

- And take *the helmet of salvation* (Know how protective your salvation is for you.)

- And *the sword of the Spirit*, which is the word of God (It becomes a weapon against the enemy when you etch it in your mind and heart.)

- *Praying always with all prayer* and supplication in the Spirit (Pray about everything.)

- *Being watchful* to this end with all perseverance and supplication for all the saints (Pray for others.)

This is not as hard as it may sound because you stand strong in *God's power* and not your own. You don't have to do everything because Jesus already did everything. Why did Jesus teach us to pray, "Deliver us from the evil one" (Matthew 6:13)? The reason is because even though Jesus accomplished the victory over evil, the enemy is still here. You don't want to be like people who can't "escape the snare of the devil, having been taken captive by him to do his will" (2 Timothy 2:26). Learn how Jesus not only defeated the enemy on the cross, but He has also given you and me—and all who receive Him into their heart and mind—the *authority* in Jesus' name to stand strong against the enemy.

His Prayer

Lord, thank You for teaching us in Your Word about the spiritual warfare we must wage against Your enemy and the enemy of our souls. We see from Your Word that we have an evil spiritual enemy, and we must always stand strong against evil. We know You will enable us to do that if we put in the effort to live Your way. Your ways are not burdensome. They are freeing and strengthening. Help us to trust in You at all times. Teach us to always do the right thing, and when we are not sure what that is, lead us when we ask You to. Enable us to be in Your Word every day so we don't lose strength and become unprepared without one of our greatest weapons. Train us to be strong in faith so we don't fall into doubt. Help us to see the truth from *Your perspective* so we are able to distinguish truth from lies of the enemy.

You laid down Your life for us. Help us to lay down our lives for You in love, obedience, prayer, worship, and total surrender to Your will and Your ways. It's not in *our strength* but in *Your power*. We realize that we wrestle against "the rulers of the darkness of this age, against spiritual *hosts* of wickedness in the heavenly *places*" (Ephesians 6:12). We praise You, Jesus, as our almighty, all-powerful King. Because You are our rock to stand on, we cannot be shaken. Thank You that You are "a shield to all who trust" in You (Psalm 18:30).

In Jesus' name I pray.

Personal Prayer Needs

_____

_____

Her Prayer

Lord, we praise You as our Deliverer and Protector because our enemies will "fall and perish at Your presence" (Psalm 9:3). Teach us to put on the whole armor of God each day and understand fully what that means. Help us to also know clearly what Your salvation did for us. Protect our minds from the lies of the enemy, who wants us to question the truth of all You have accomplished for us. Enable us to put on the helmet of salvation which promotes the renewing of our mind so we can be transformed and not confused.

Help us to recognize and deliberately put on the sword of the Spirit, which is the truth of Your Word. We know it is a double-edged sword in our hands, and it is one of our most valuable and greatest weapons. Fill our hearts and minds with Your Word so that we remember and retain it completely and are able to stand strong in it without wavering. Make us strong in You so that we stand strong in faith without doubting. Keep us from ever giving up. Let that never be an option to us. Draw us into total unity about this so that we never display weakness. Enable us to continue to pray with Your guidance so we see great things happen.

Thank You, Lord, that You are our defender, and You will fight for us (see Psalm 7:10). And when each battle is over, we will be able to say that this was the Lord's doing, and it is marvelous in our eyes (see Psalm 118:23).

In Jesus' name I pray.

Personal Prayer Needs

_____

_____

TRUTH TO AGREE ON

Be strong in the Lord and in the power of His might.
Put on the whole armor of God,
that you may be able to stand against the wiles of the devil.
For we do not wrestle against flesh and blood,
but against principalities, against powers,
against the rulers of darkness of this age,
against spiritual hosts of wickedness in the heavenly places.

EPHESIANS 6:10-12

Ask, and it will be given to you; seek, and you will find;
knock, and it will be opened to you.
For everyone who asks receives, and he who seeks finds,
and to him who knocks it will be opened.

LUKE 11:9-10

Delight yourself also in the LORD,
and He shall give you the desires of your heart.

PSALM 37:4

Be steadfast, immovable, always abounding
in the work of the Lord,
knowing that your labor is not in vain in the Lord.

1 CORINTHIANS 15:58

CHAPTER 18

Surviving Pain in Times of Loss

t's quite possible we all will go through painful times of loss in our lives. The worst is the unbearable loss of a loved one, and especially the heartbreaking loss of a child. How does anyone survive that? We all hope and pray that we and others will never have to experience anything like that, but many of us do. Things happen. People die. Some losses are harder than others. Some are unbearable, and we cannot go through them alone without the comfort of other strong believers around us. And not without the loving, healing, comforting, life-changing presence of God.

Great loss can also come from a crippling disease or injury. It can be a divorce, which is the death of a dream that once was. A child who strays to experience severe consequences for their mistakes is a painful experience. The disastrous loss of a home and perhaps everything in it. The sudden loss of finances or a high-valued job, neither of which you saw coming so you were not at all prepared. With some of these losses you can still feel hopeful about the future, and you can agree together and say, "It's okay. We'll get through this." Other losses are so unbearable you may wonder how you can get through another minute, another hour, or one more day. When you grieve the unexpected loss of a close person, it is so final that it is hard to envision a future without them. Your life, as you once knew it, seems forever destroyed. These losses can bring such pain that you don't know how you can survive them. And you wonder if you will ever feel anything but that horrible pain. Will there be a time when you feel normal again?

While all the words and deeds of kindness from friends and family mean a lot, you can't rely on them to say the exact thing you need that will bring the healing you long for. It's unfair to expect people to say the perfect words, especially when they have not experienced the loss you have. We have to see the love and care in people's hearts who have come to comfort us, however perfectly or awkwardly that comfort is offered.

And everyone grieves differently. The same is true with you and your husband or wife. You have to extend grace to let him or her grieve their own way. Some want to be alone. Some need to be with others. The worst thing to do in this time of loss is to blame your husband or wife for what happened. It's devastating enough without being blamed for it. No one is able to bear that kind of judgment. It can destroy a marriage quickly. No one can survive it.

People can comfort us, but only God can take that pain away over time. That doesn't mean you don't grieve for a long time, or even a lifetime, but there can come a day when you can have some time away from feeling that horrible sense of loss. There can even be moments of joy.

Whatever you do, don't fall into the trap of blaming God for what happened. It is a dead-end street to close yourself off from the very source that can one day take your pain away and bring healing. Keep in mind that God is always good, and our enemy (who is God's enemy too) is always seeking to kill and destroy. Keep seeking God's presence in your life. Determine to walk with Him through each minute, hour, and day even when it seems your pain will never end. Agree together to seek God's restoration and healing, and stand in faith that He promises to *bless* those who *mourn* and *comfort* them (see Matthew 5:4).

The Bible also promises, "The people who walked in darkness have seen a great light; those who dwelt in the land of the shadow of death, upon them a light has shined" (Isaiah 9:2). Our lives will not always have this dark shadow of grief over us. His light will shine on us and dispel that horrible darkness. And you can believe that your mourning will end.

His Prayer

Lord, we praise You that You will comfort us in our darkest hour of loss. We can depend on You to keep us from suffering forever from any great loss we may experience. Where our hearts are hurting now in a way that seems endless to us, we pray that You will one day take our pain away. Lift us out of hopelessness. We put our hope in You because You are always faithful to help us recover.

If we don't have any point of great loss at this time, we ask that You would protect us from any disaster that would be hard to bear. But if loss or great disappointment does happen, we ask You to carry us through it to restoration and healing. Keep us aware of whatever we need to do to avoid disasters and the plans of the enemy. If there is anything we can do to prevent painful loss, show us. No matter what happens, keep us from blaming one another, or You, for whatever happens. Help us recognize whatever hand the enemy of our souls has had in any tragedy instead.

If either of us has blamed the other already, help us to confess it to You. If we have mistakenly blamed You for allowing a tragedy to happen, we confess that now before You as a grave error and ask Your forgiveness. Keep us from ever doing that. We know You are a good God, and You love us and want only what is best for us. Be merciful to us because we trust You, we take refuge in You, and we know You will pour on us Your mercy and truth (see Psalm 57:1-3).

In Jesus' name I pray.

Personal Prayer Needs

_____

_____

Her Prayer

Praise You, Lord, that You are our Comforter in times of loss. We pray there will never be any devastating loss in our lives, something we feel we cannot recover from the pain of it. Protect us in that way. But if anything like that ever does happen, help us to comfort one another and not blame the other. Especially keep us from ever blaming You because we think You should prevent every painful thing that happens to us. You would not have promised to bless and comfort those who mourn if You did not know we would need that (see Matthew 5:4).

We lift up to You any loss either of us has experienced that is still terribly painful and overwhelming in our life now. Only You can fill the empty and hurting place in our hearts and bring healing. When we feel as though we cannot live through the pain of our loss or great disappointment, we know You will sustain us.

Thank You, Lord, that Your Word says *You* have "borne our griefs and carried our sorrows" (Isaiah 53:4). No matter what happens, You see us through. You are our light in the midst of dark times. Thank You that Your Word gives us life, especially when we are afflicted by grief (see Psalm 119:50).

Lord, we worship You as our precious Redeemer. We praise You for Your restoration from any grief or sadness that we carry in our hearts now or *will* carry in the future. We put our hope in You, for with You there is mercy (see Psalm 130:7).

In Jesus' name I pray.

Personal Prayer Needs

_____

_____

TRUTH TO AGREE ON

Blessed are those who mourn,
for they shall be comforted.

MATTHEW 5:4

This is my comfort in my affliction,
for Your word has given me life.

PSALM 119:50

The LORD will be your everlasting light,
and the days of your mourning shall be ended.

ISAIAH 60:20

You number my wanderings;
put my tears into Your bottle;
are they not in Your book?
When I cry out to You,
then my enemies will turn back;
this I know, because God is for me.

PSALM 56:8-9

These things I have spoken to you,
that in Me you may have peace.
In the world you will have tribulation;
but be of good cheer, I have overcome the world.

JOHN 16:33

CHAPTER 19

Walking in the Joy of the Lord

We all need joy in our lives. The Bible says, "The joy of the LORD is your strength" (Nehemiah 8:10). The joy that comes from knowing and loving God is greater than anything we will ever find in the flesh. That's because it has its root in God. It's deeper and more life giving than anything we can conjure up on our own. It happens when His Spirit of joy is poured in us. Nothing on earth gives us a source of constant joy the way He can. But we have to spend time with Him, inviting Him into our life every day, seeking Him and depending on Him to fulfill us. When we silently demand that our spouse do that for us, it can be overwhelming to him or her.

I never experienced true joy until I found it in the Lord. I have described it in another book as feeling like a sunrise has risen in your heart. It is gentle, warm, strengthening, healing, illuminating, and a complete end in itself. You need nothing more in that moment. It's what I think we will feel when we go to be with the Lord—only our joy will be even greater than anything we will ever feel on earth. When you feel it, you are content to bask in the blessing. Once you experience it, you don't want to ever let anything try to rob you of the joy God has for you.

Jesus said, "He who believes in Me, as the Scripture has said, out of his heart will flow rivers of living water" (John 7:38). Those rivers that bring love, joy, and peace are connected to the Holy Spirit. God is love. His joy rises in us to give us strength. And He gives us peace beyond what we can ever imagine. We can have both strength and joy in our heart no matter what is going on in our life. We experience a deep sense of His presence.

Whenever you feel you have lost your joy because of life's circumstances, seek the Lord for *His* joy. Ask for it, pray for it, wait for it. It can rise in your heart when you least expect it. He has it for you. Invite His Holy Spirit to rise in you and give you that supernatural strength He has promised to those who seek Him with all their heart. He has it for you right now for the asking.

The joy of the Lord is a gift He gives us when we seek to find our joy in Him. The joy He gives us happens no matter what else is happening *around* and *in* us, and this joy is greater than any joy we can ever find by ourselves without Him. His joy is perfect. You need nothing else in those moments.

The Bible says of joy, "You will show me the path of life; in Your presence is fullness of joy; at Your right hand are pleasures forevermore" (Psalm 16:11). The Bible says we should look to Jesus, "who for the joy that was set before Him endured the cross" and went to be with God to sit at His right hand forever (Hebrews 12:2). No matter how it feels right now or next year, joy is in your future when you walk with the Lord and live to be in His presence.

God's love, peace, and joy happen in your life when you long to be in God's presence. The joy of the Lord rises in you like a ray of warm sunshine on a cold day. It's like an endless spring of pure water that quenches your thirst for more of Him in your heart, mind, and soul. When you worship and praise Him, that joy comes from an endless source. You experience a joy that makes you feel as though you are lifted above whatever is happening around you, and He will never leave you nor forsake you.

The Bible says God tells us to "be still and know that I am God" (Psalm 46:10). There are times when we just need to be in God's presence. We let go of everything else to be with Him. Who doesn't need that?

His Prayer

Lord, thank You that You have promised to give us joy that will rise in us and become our strength—especially when we feel that we don't have strength enough to cope with whatever we are facing. We worship You and long to experience Your presence. "How lovely *is* Your tabernacle, O LORD of hosts! My soul longs, yes, even faints for the courts of the LORD; my heart and my flesh cry out for the living God" (Psalm 84:1-2).

Help us to experience Your joy rising in us every time we worship You—alone or together. Thank You for Your Word that says, "In Your presence is fullness of joy" (Psalm 16:11). You have said, "All who seek the LORD will praise him. Their hearts will rejoice with everlasting joy" (Psalm 22:26 NLT). I say, according to Your Word, "By Him let us continually offer the sacrifice of praise to God, that is, the fruit of our lips, giving thanks to His name" (Hebrews 13:15).

Thank You that You have said about the future in Your Word, "Behold, I make all things new" (Revelation 21:5).

Lord, we want to show our love for You through our worship and adoration. We want to bless You at all times and have Your praise continually be in our minds, in our thoughts, and in the words we speak (see Psalm 34:1). You are everything to us, and we want to serve You with joy in our hearts.

In Jesus' name I pray.

Personal Prayer Needs

_____

_____

Her Prayer

Lord, You are worthy to be praised and worshipped every day of our lives. Enable my husband and me to seek You wholeheartedly many times each day, even when we are not together in the same room. We ask that when we do pray together, that Your joy will rise in our hearts to become our source of strength. Thank You that the joy You give us is always healing and rejuvenating—especially in times when we have grown weary.

We know that in Your presence we will find everything we will ever need. We long to know all there is to know about You. We want our worship of You to be like the air we breathe. We want to show our love for You with our worship of You. We know that our wholehearted worship of You—which leads us into receiving the fullness of Your joy—is the closest we will ever be to You in this life.

Thank You for Your Word that says even though we may weep for a dark season, Your joy will come in the morning (see Psalm 30:5). Your Word says that we are to keep Your commandments in order to abide in Your love, just as Jesus kept Your commandments and abided in Your love. You spoke these words so that Your joy would remain in those who love You and that our joy would be full (see John 15:10-11). Nothing would give us more joy than to please You.

In Jesus' name I pray.

Personal Prayer Needs

_____

_____

TRUTH TO AGREE ON

May the God of hope fill you
with all joy and peace in believing,
that you may abound in hope
by the power of the Holy Spirit.

ROMANS 15:13

Count it all joy when you fall into various trials,
knowing that the testing of your faith produces patience.

JAMES 1:2-3

Weeping may endure for a night,
but joy comes in the morning.

PSALM 30:5

You have turned for me my mourning into dancing;
You have put off my sackcloth and clothed me with gladness.

PSALM 30:11

His lord said to him, "Well done, good and faithful servant;
you were faithful over a few things,
I will make you ruler over many things.
Enter into the joy of your lord."

MATTHEW 25:21

CHAPTER 20

Staying Faithful to the End

One of the main things that grieved God about the Israelites is that they didn't stay true to Him. He was doing major miracles for them and leading them to a place of blessing, but they lost faith every time they faced a challenge. They did not have the heart to stay faithful to the one, true, living God—nor to His ways and His Word. They kept going after false gods and worshipping dead idols even after all the miracles God did on their behalf. God hates when people aren't true to Him. And He hates it just as much when a person in a marriage is not true to his or her spouse.

Living loosely with staying true to the Lord—or your spouse— is never acceptable and will always plant a terrible seed that will grow a crop of bad fruit in your life. You have probably already decided that you will do all that is necessary to stay true to your husband or wife, and you have chosen to live true to the Lord in your life as well. That is a good thing because you cannot claim the promises of God for yourself and your marriage if there is any entertaining of infidelity on the side, even in your mind. God sees it all. Just the thought of that must be confessed and crushed immediately when it comes to mind. You may have never thought of being unfaithful to your spouse or to the Lord in your life, but surely the enemy of your soul has thought of it for you, and he would like to lure you away from the ways of God for both you and your spouse.

It's possible to avoid anything like that by praying to God about what you will not allow into your mind and heart. You must be knowledgeable about God's Word concerning your relationship with Him and your relationship with your husband or wife. It starts with a wholehearted decision you make that you will be faithful to God and faithful to your husband or wife. You declare both of these things before the Lord and before your spouse. And then you ask the Lord to help you to always be true in your heart to both. You need to pray that you will not be led into temptation by the enemy, but you will be delivered from evil, just as God told us to pray (see Matthew 6:9-13).

The Bible says, "The eyes of the LORD run to and fro throughout the whole earth, to show Himself strong on behalf of those whose heart is loyal to Him" (2 Chronicles 16:9). God is looking for people who will be loyal to Him so He can show Himself strong on their behalf. We all need to be on His side if we want to witness His miraculous power.

The Bible says, "The lamp of the body is the eye. If therefore your eye is good, your whole body will be full of light. But if your eye is bad, your whole body will be full of darkness. If therefore the light that is in you is darkness, how great is that darkness!" (Matthew 6:22-23). We must keep track of what we allow our eyes to see. If we look at the dark side and are drawn to it, we can become the biggest losers, and our losses can last for a lifetime. There is something great in deciding to stay faithful to God and to one another until the end of our life. God's Word says, "Why should you, my son, be enraptured by an immoral woman, and be embraced in the arms of a seductress? For the ways of man are before the eyes of the LORD, and He ponders all his paths" (Proverbs 5:20-21).

God sees everything whether we think so or not. We cannot escape His all-knowing and all-seeing capabilities. Instead, God says for the best outcome, we need to follow these suggestions: "My son, give attention to my words; incline your ear to my sayings. Do not let them depart from your eyes; keep them in the midst of your heart; for they are life to those who find them, and health to all their flesh. *Keep your heart with all diligence,* for out of it spring the issues of life. Put away from you a *deceitful mouth,* and put *perverse lips* far from you. Let your eyes look straight ahead, and your eyelids look right before you. Ponder the path of your feet, and let all your ways be established. Do not turn to the right or the left; remove your foot from evil" (Proverbs 4:20-27).

His Prayer

Lord, we praise You that You will lead us in the ways we should walk when each of us lifts up our heart, soul, mind, and body to You. We ask according to Your Word that we will not be led into temptation, but that You will deliver us from the evil one (see Matthew 6:9-13). We want nothing to do with the enemy in our life. We do not want to be led astray by his deception.

I pray my wife and I will always serve You loyally and truthfully to the end of our lives here on earth. Help us to stay in Your Word in order to be reminded how much You hate it when we are not honest with You and with one another. Always keep us from deception in our relationship with You, and never allow us to be diverted away by the enemy's enticement, even in thoughts about our love for each other.

You know our path far better than we can figure it out on our own. Teach us to walk with You every day so that You can take us where we need to go. Help us to not lean on our own understanding, but to trust You with all our heart so that You can direct our path (see Proverbs 3:5-6). We don't want to go off on our own path. We want to stay faithful to Your way right to the end.

In Jesus' name I pray.

Personal Prayer Needs

_____

_____

Her Prayer

Lord, we praise You for Your promises to us. Help us to always draw near to You so that You will continually draw near to us (see James 4:8). Help us to never forget Your Word that promises the nearness of Your presence.

Help us to never feel as though we are failing if we have to depend on You to get where we need to be. Teach us to always see that our risk for failure goes up if we don't depend on You. Enable us to know for certain that we cannot take steps without depending on You every day. Help us to be eager to follow You because we know You will do great things through us.

We don't want to take one step without You, so if we have gotten off the path You have for us in any way, make a path now from where we are to where we need to be and help us to stay on it. Take us where we need to go.

Thank You, Lord God, that You love us so much. Nothing can ever separate us from Your love. Your love lasts forever, and because You *are* love and Your love is *in* us, *our love* for one another can *last forever* as well. Deepen and strengthen our love for You every day. We lift our hearts up to You. Pour Your love into both of us.

In Jesus' name I pray.

Personal Prayer Needs

_____

_____

TRUTH TO AGREE ON

I have come as a light into the world,
that whoever believes in Me
should not abide in darkness.

JOHN 12:46

The path of the just is like the shining sun,
that shines ever brighter unto the perfect day.

PROVERBS 4:18

A man's heart plans his way,
but the Lord directs his steps.

PROVERBS 16:9

Be faithful until death,
and I will give you the crown of life.

REVELATION 2:10

Cause me to know the way
in which I should walk,
for I lift up my soul to You.

PSALM 143:8

CHAPTER 21

Raising Children Together

Raising children together means you must come to many agreements as to what you will and will not allow into their lives and minds, and in your house. This is an extremely important area to agree on. A united front is much more powerful to your children than you might think. This means teaching them who God is and what He says about *them* and *you* as parents.

It doesn't matter what age your children are—from birth to as long as you are alive—they need your prayers. It's very important to ask God to help you rely on Him to teach you what is right and good and what is not as you raise them each day.

As a married couple, you must agree on *having* children, *raising* children, and *disciplining* children. (Even if you are no longer married, you two are still their parents and will need to agree on important matters regarding them.) Ask God to help you show the love of Jesus to them so well that they will grow to *love Him* more than they love anyone or anything else. Teach by your example together. Pray with them about everything that concerns them. Be certain in your mind and heart that your prayers for your child or children will be the most powerful influence in their lives.

First of all, if you have not done this already, deliberately dedicate each child's life to the Lord. Say, "Lord, we dedicate this child to You and Your kingdom for Your purposes. Be in charge of him or her and bless all growth and development. Teach us what we need to do and how to pray." Do it in a church service designed for that, or do it alone as a family. You may be ruled by worry and fear if either of you is not sure that God is in control of your child's life. This doesn't mean that nothing can ever go wrong because he or she will still have a choice about what he or she *will* and *will not* do, and he or she may have to suffer the consequences if he or she makes a bad choice. Nothing makes you feel more like a failure than when something goes wrong in your child's life. Your guilt over what you feel might be caused by your own failure is very painful. Just remember that you don't have to be a *perfect* parent, but you do need to be a faithful *praying* parent. And that is something you *can* do.

When you pray about everything concerning your children, God will carry that burden along with you and give you wisdom, power, and ability far beyond yourselves to see great things happen in them. Don't leave your children's lives to chance by neglecting to pray for them. This is true no matter how young or old they are. It is never too *late* or too *early* to start *praying* for your children, or to *teach your children* to *pray*.

When your children are adults, don't think your prayers for them are over. They may be on their own, but evil will lurk around them, and they will need your prayers covering them and claiming them for God's kingdom and purposes. It is still a very important calling to be in agreement about how you pray for your adult children. God's power in you *together* will be far stronger if you two are in *unity* about this.

God has given you spiritual authority over your young children. This doesn't mean there will always be an immediate answer to your prayers. Depending on their age or level of obedience, what they have in their hearts toward you and toward God is very important. Be in agreement about how to pray for each one.

Remember, your prayers are never meaningless. If you are praying, something is always happening, so don't become discouraged and stop praying. Your prayers—as you *agree*—are very powerful. Even if you don't quickly see the changes you want to see, just keep loving your children and praying for them, and they will see the hand of God moving in their parents and their own life. That will account for a lot.

Your adult children still need the power of two praying together in unity about the things they might not think to pray about for themselves. For example, praying that they will develop a heart for the things of God and His Word, praying they will resist evil, praying they will grow in God's wisdom and discernment, and praying they will have a sense of God's purpose for their life. You have no idea how much grief you will spare them when you pray for these things. You will never spoil them with too much prayer. It's not possible.

His Prayer

Lord, we praise You for any children or grandchildren You give us—both now or in the future. We know that children are a gift from You, and we are always grateful to You for them. We know we aren't *perfect* parents, but we *can* be *praying* parents. Help us to agree on that and teach us how to pray in Your name every day for them. Show us specifics about how to pray for each one of them.

Help us to come to an agreement about how our children will be raised, and about what is acceptable behavior and what is not. We know our prayers together in unity are more powerful because we pray in Your name. Keep us always praying for them no matter how old they are or how old we are.

Help us to agree on what we should say, read, and pray that will help our children to develop a hunger for Your Word and ways. Help us to find the best church for our children and teens that draws them closer to You and attracted to godly friends.

We pray for any children or grandchildren we have that there is surely "a future hope" for them and their "hope will not be cut off" because You are their heavenly Father (Proverbs 23:18 NIV). Even if we don't have any of our own natural or adopted children, show us any child in our lives who would benefit from our prayers for their expressed needs.

In Jesus' name I pray.

Personal Prayer Needs

Her Prayer

Lord, I pray You will lead my husband and me in the right way, especially in raising our children, any grandchildren we may have in our future, or any children who may come into our lives. Help us to agree on how we should raise them and how we relate to them when they are grown. We know there will never be a time when they do not need our prayers. Cause them to always be drawn toward You and Your ways. Help my husband and me to help them develop a deep love and gratitude toward You. Enable us to teach them to be responsible, sensitive, loving, compassionate, and giving people, especially toward You and toward us. Make them to be worshippers of You. Give them a hunger for more of You so they will spend time in worship, prayer, praise, and in learning about Your ways. Give them a teachable heart that says yes to the things of God and no to the things of evil or selfish desires.

We put our children in Your hands, and we ask You to be Lord and Savior to them. Help them to learn who You are at an early age. Help us to always reflect Your love to them in ways that are clearly perceivable.

In Jesus' name I pray.

Personal Prayer Needs

_____

_____

TRUTH TO AGREE ON

Pour out your heart like water before the face of the Lord.
Lift your hands toward Him for the life of your young children.

LAMENTATIONS 2:19

Children, obey your parents in the Lord, for this is right.
"Honor your father and mother,"
which is the first commandment with promise:
"that it may be well with you and you may live long on the earth."
And you, fathers, do not provoke your children to wrath,
but bring them up in the training and admonition of the Lord.

EPHESIANS 6:1-4

Whatever you ask in My name, that I will do,
that the Father may be glorified in the Son.

JOHN 14:13

Cursed is the one who treats his father or his mother
with contempt.

DEUTERONOMY 27:16

Blessed are those who keep His testimonies,
who seek Him with the whole heart!

PSALM 119:2

CHAPTER 22

Following God's Leading

Some of the most beautiful verses in the Bible come from the words Jesus spoke about His believers. He said, "My *sheep* hear My *voice*, and I *know* them, and they *follow* Me. And I give them eternal life, and they shall never perish; neither shall anyone snatch them out of My hand. My Father, who has given *them* to Me, is greater than all; and no one is able to snatch *them* out of My Father's hand" (John 10:27-29). What an amazing promise to those of us who know Jesus, love Him, and follow His leading every day. You can hear His voice in your heart and follow Him in everything if you ask Him to help you do so. He gives you eternal life so you will never die. And God, who has given the true believers His Son, will *never lose* them. They can never be taken from Him. God is greater than everything and every person, so nothing and no one can ever take you away from God.

We must follow God's leading every day. We must seek His will and His way and know what those are at all times. This is a safety tool. When we seek to specifically know His leading and follow Him, He gives us great and perfect instruction. Praise God for His perfect will for you. Thank Him that you can always know it. Thank Him for whatever direction He gives You and *will* give you.

Somewhere in the midst of your praying, praising, and worshipping Him, He will reveal Himself and His will to you. Thank Him that He is a God who can be known. He wants you to know Him and to know His will for your life. He wants to reveal His will to you so you can make the decisions you need to make together in perfect unity because you have both heard God impress certain things upon your hearts in the same way. If you find you still don't agree on something, keep praying about how you can come to an agreement. Often it is the very act of praising and worshipping Him for His all-knowing capability that will bring you revelation of His will and His specific leading.

Anyone who *wants* to *know* Him better *can* and *will*. God will reveal much to you as you read His Word. You can find things there that are always God's will for your life. For example, it is always God's will that you love each other and also that you love others. It is always God's will to worship Him.

Whenever you need to know God's direction regarding certain things, ask Him and He will show you. He has promised that those who have received His Son, Jesus, have the mind of Christ (see 1 Corinthians 2:16). What an amazing gift. Don't forget that. There will be times when the enemy will try to convince you otherwise, and you need to confirm the opposite and say, "Thank You, God, that I have the mind of Christ." Agree on that together. Your greatest joy and peace will be found when you are in the will of God. You have to agree together in order to achieve that. You both need to want God's will more than your own.

However, there are things God wants you to know every day as He leads you specifically in your life together. Always ask Him to show you whatever you need to see for you and your family. Don't make any decision without checking in with God and your spouse as to what that decision should be. It's important to be correct on that because being wrong on any of the decisions you have to make can cause a major setback. Think of any decision you need to make today or that you know you are going to have to make in your future. Pray to know the Lord's leading on everything now, and don't think you don't need to. Being wrong about this can be very costly in every way.

Remember that God will supply all your needs, but you first must acknowledge your need before Him. Paul said, "I have learned in whatever state I am, to be content" (Philippians 4:11). The reason Paul could say that is because he knew his need was always for more of God.

His Prayer

Lord, we thank You that You are the God of the universe and You can be known. Thank You that You share Yourself with us, and You share Your will with us about our lives because You want us to know *You*. Your desire is for us to follow Your leading every day because You love us and You always know what is best for us. Thank You that Your will for us will always be a place of blessing.

Holy Spirit, lead us in Your will and Your ways every day. We give You permission to perfect in us the complete surrender of our lives to You. Fill us with the knowledge of Your will. Direct our steps so we don't stumble away from the path You have for us. Help us to talk clearly with each other about any fears we have concerning missing what You are leading us to. Help us to never misunderstand Your leading or move too quickly, thinking we know best.

Silence every voice in our lives that is not from You. Keep us from ever falling into deception. Keep us from loving the world's spirit more than Your Spirit. Teach us how to look to You for guidance about each decision we make. Enable us to always seek You as our guide. Keep us from ever thinking we can live without Your input every day. Help us to depend on You for every step we take.

In Jesus' name I pray.

Personal Prayer Needs

_____

_____

Her Prayer

Lord, I praise You as the all-knowing Creator of the universe and God of our lives. We trust You for all the knowledge we will ever need. We rely on You and not ourselves to give us insight regarding the things we need to know. I know it is always Your will for us to give thanks to You in all things, but wherever there are specific things we need to pray about, enable us to always see that so we will seek to know *Your* leading in our lives.

I know it is Your will that we would rejoice always, pray without ceasing, and in everything give thanks to You (see 1 Thessalonians 5:16-18). Help us to remember that worshipping and praising You is crucial when we need to know Your leading for our lives. Impart Your knowledge to us so we can understand Your perfect guidance. Give us hearts that are willing to receive all You have for us and to agree in unity of spirit. Give us ears to hear what You are speaking to our hearts at all times.

Work in us what is well pleasing in Your sight (see Hebrews 13:21). We don't want to think we know everything about what You are leading us to do or not do. Give us the endurance we need to do the right thing so we never miss what that is and forfeit all You have for us. Thank You, Lord, that You will preserve our going out and our coming in from this time forth (see Psalm 121:8).

In Jesus' name I pray.

Personal Prayer Needs

_____

_____

TRUTH TO AGREE ON

Your ears shall hear a word behind you, saying,
"This is the way, walk in it,"
whenever you turn to the right hand
or whenever you turn to the left.

ISAIAH 30:21

Do not be conformed to this world,
but be transformed by the renewing of your mind,
that you may prove what is that good and acceptable
and perfect will of God.

ROMANS 12:2

The world is passing away, and the lust of it;
but he who does the will of God abides forever.

1 JOHN 2:17

Not everyone who says to Me, "Lord, Lord,"
shall enter the kingdom of heaven,
but he who does the will of My Father in heaven.

MATTHEW 7:21

We also…do not cease to pray for you,
and to ask that you may be filled
with the knowledge of His will.

COLOSSIANS 1:9

CHAPTER 23

Avoiding the Pitfalls

There can be many pitfalls in a marriage relationship you don't expect and definitely never want to fall into. But I believe they are a setup by the enemy of your souls and your marriage designed specifically to do damage. At the very least, they don't end up well, but there are ways to avoid them absolutely.

The Bible says there are certain things we should never do, and we need to heed those. For example, if you claim to love your spouse and have committed yourself to him or her in your marriage vows, then the things the Lord says *not* to do to someone you love will become very clear. The Bible says if you lack patience or kindness, or if you are callous, prideful, easily irritated, and want what you want every moment you want it, then you do not really have love (see 1 Corinthians 13). Anyone of those things is a pitfall you can stumble into in your marriage, and they can lead to many hurtful situations that could easily be avoided. When you finally see the damage that can be done, you will regret not praying about those things together.

What the Bible says specifically about love is that it "does not behave rudely, does not seek its own, is not provoked, thinks no evil; does not rejoice in iniquity, but rejoices in the truth; bears all things, believes all things, hopes all things, endures all things" (1 Corinthians 13:5-7).

So, if you don't allow yourself to entertain any evil thoughts, if you refuse to be smug when bad things happen, if you never think of telling lies as an option, if you have *patience* with the imperfections of your spouse, if you believe in and hope for the best in your husband or wife, and if you choose to not always be thinking of yourself, then you will avoid deep pitfalls, your love will not fail, and you can have a marriage that lasts a lifetime.

One of the things Jesus said is that you shouldn't worry about anything because God knows what you need (see Matthew 6:31-32). But He didn't say to never pray about the things that concern you. And another thing He said was to not be deceived (see James 1:6). He would not have said that if He didn't know we could be, and we have a choice about it. Actually, I've heard some Christian speakers and writers clearly say that if we don't think we can be deceived, then we already are. That is a very scary thought, and it made me want to pray for both my husband and myself more than ever.

In order to stay undeceived, we have to spend time with God, getting to know Him and His ways well and being very suspicious of what we think is our ability to stand strong against deception. We must ask Him to help us to clearly be able to distinguish between the truth and a lie. We have to seek God first above all things (see Matthew 6:33).

The truth is, it's far too easy for the enemy to believe he can deceive us into thinking that we can never be deceived. How many times have we seen a person we would never in a million years think would cheat on their husband or wife, and we are shocked to hear when it happens. All it takes is enough pride to enter into the deceived person and cause him or her to believe he or she is above God's laws. Don't let that ever be you or your spouse. Pray about this often so that your first priority is always to seek the Lord.

When the Bible talks about how you should love your neighbor as yourself, that is not so easy to do (see Matthew 22:39). We need God's help. If you can remember that your husband or wife is your closest neighbor, that will help. If we keep that in mind, we won't mindlessly go off the deep end in our marriage right into a pitfall that is very hard to climb out of. Ask God to show you what *love does* and *does not* do. We really have to get this straight.

His Prayer

Lord, thank You that every time my wife and I worship You, You show Yourself to be greater than we can imagine. It never fails that Your love toward us is far greater than any we can ever hope to imitate. Thank You that Your ways always work for our benefit. Thank You that You protect us from the plans of the enemy. Thank You that we must seek You above all things in order to not fall into deception. Your Word says we must not deceive ourselves and think we can never become deceived because the enemy lays up traps for us to fall into as a married couple. We don't ever want to fall into those made-for-destruction scenarios that our flesh might find easy to buy into but are very hard to repair once we do.

We ask that You keep us from falling into those "love does not do this" signs in Your Word. Keep my wife and me from being rude to one another. Give each of us patience with the other. Help us to confess quickly whenever we find that we have let ourselves become more concerned with what *we* want over what *You* want. Keep us from ever being deceived by the enemy of our souls, who is known as the great deceiver. Lead us to clearly see Your truth so we will keep from falling into deception. Help us to faithfully read Your Word so that we will not fall prey to the enemy's lies and land up in the pit prepared for our destruction. Help us to quickly see the truth about ourselves if we ever step off the path You have for us.

In Jesus' name I pray.

Personal Prayer Needs

_____

_____

Her Prayer

Lord, thank You that You are the God of the universe who knows and sees everything. Thank You that You know when we are getting near the edge where we can be influenced by the deceiver. Keep us safe from ever falling under his spell. Show us clearly when we start believing lies and not Your truth. We want to seek You first in all things.

Give both my husband and me patience and kindness toward one another. Keep us from being easily irritated. Help us instead to believe good things about each other. Keep us always close to You and Your truth and far from the lies of the enemy. Enable us to always think of how the other one feels in response to the words we say. Your love is the greatest of all because it lasts forever and never fails. And that is because You are love and You will never fail. Help us "pursue love" in our marriage relationship (see 1 Corinthians 14:1).

Remind us that we become more like You when we draw near and walk close to You. We pray specifically that You will keep us from thinking we can become prideful without serious consequences. Keep us growing in Your ways so that we never allow ourselves to become unteachable because we think we know it all.

In Jesus' name I pray.

Personal Prayer Needs

_____

_____

TRUTH TO AGREE ON

Now abide faith, hope, love, these three;
but the greatest of these is love.

1 CORINTHIANS 13:13

Let us not grow weary while doing good,
for in due season we shall reap if we do not lose heart.

GALATIANS 6:9

O God, You are my God; early will I seek You;
my soul thirsts for You; my flesh longs for You
in a dry and thirsty land where there is no water.

PSALM 63:1

The day of the Lord will come as a thief in the night,
in which the heavens will pass away with a great noise,
and the elements will melt with fervent heat;
both the earth and the works that are in it will be burned up.
Therefore, since all these things will be dissolved,
what manner of persons ought you to be in
holy conduct and godliness.

2 PETER 3:10-11

CHAPTER 24

Enduring Hard Times

Make no mistake. God allows those He loves to go through hard times. It happens to everyone at some point. It's not that God stops loving us. In fact, quite the opposite. He loves us so much that He is not going to keep us from ever experiencing anything difficult because He wants our faith in Him to grow. He desires that our faith and knowledge of Him will sustain us. He wants us to know what it means to trust Him even when we see no way out of what we are going through.

One of the first steps of faith required by us is to learn how to walk in the light of His truth. We must learn great lessons of faith from His Word, for then He will teach us how to walk through dark times with the comfort of His presence as our only light.

Also, it's in the dark and difficult times, when you experience the comfort of His light with you, that will cause you to long for His presence every moment of your life. If you have been walking a crooked path—or a kind of hit-and-miss meandering—He will show you a straight path to walk with Him. If you are going in the wrong direction, He will turn you around. When you stop whatever you are doing and ask Him to show you if you are going

in the right direction, He will lead you to where you are supposed
to be. So many times it is *not God* who has let go of *us*. It is *we*
who have let go of *Him*. But even so, every time we reach up for
Him in prayer and worship, He is always there to receive us back
to Himself.

Sometimes, however, you are not going through a hard time
in your life because you have done something wrong, but rather
because you are doing something right. And it's very important
to see what the truth is about that. God may just be teaching you
how to trust Him in the difficult times. Or He wants to take you
to a new place you have never been before with Him, where He
can help you learn how great the depth of His love is for you. He
wants you to let Him lift you up far above where you can possibly go alone without Him. God wants you to be dependent on
Him—and that is not a sign that you are weak. It's a sign that you
can be stronger when you depend fully on Him to get you where
you need to go. God guides you on the path because you are willing to let Him lead you.

One of the things about God is that He doesn't always tell you
where you're going in your life. Abraham experienced this. "He
went out, not knowing where he was going" (Hebrews 11:8). All
of the great and godly people of the Bible had times of not knowing where God was leading. They just knew God wanted them to
trust Him wherever that was. So draw close to God, and let Him
draw you close to Him.

Hard times are made worse when you stop communicating
with your spouse. You cannot have a marriage that lasts a lifetime
without good communication. If you can pray together every day,
pray about the things you need to be honest with each other about,
such as your fears, hopes, needs, and thoughts. You have to feel
close to each other in prayer in order to feel that you are on the
same page and on the same team. This is the person with whom
you should be able to share everything, so you need to know what

each other is thinking about certain things. And are you *agreeing* or are you *not?* There cannot be too many mysteries or secrets in a marriage. There is no way you can always be there for each other if you don't talk or communicate.

Although God never changes, it's because He doesn't need to. We, on the other hand, *do* need to change. In fact, He wants you to change perhaps more than you may realize. That's because He wants so much more for each of you than you ever dreamed possible for yourselves.

His Prayer

Lord, I thank You that You are the source of everything we need. You are everything to us. Thank You that You have a plan for our lives together. I know that "the upright shall dwell in Your presence" (Psalm 140:13). Even when we are going through hard times, You are always with us because we have proclaimed You the Lord, Savior, Healer, and Deliverer of our lives.

Help us to always grow in trust for You, no matter what we are going through. Teach us to see all the blessings in our lives and praise You for them—even when we are going through the most difficult of times. We thank You that, in the day when we cried out to You, You answered us, and we became bold with strength in our soul (see Psalm 138:3). Thank You, Lord, that Your Word is a lamp for our feet and a light for our path (see Psalm 119:105). Help us to stay in Your Word so it can light our way every day.

Teach us to be honest with each other about the way we see things. Break down any barriers between us that have risen in our hearts and have been built up between us. Enable us to always remember to show our appreciation for one another. Even in hard times, keep us from ever accepting less than the life You have for us.

In Jesus' name I pray.

Personal Prayer Needs

_____

_____

Her Prayer

Thank You, Lord, that Your Word is always a light for us to help guide us where we need to go—especially when we go through difficult times. Shine light from Your Word in us today. Bring it alive in our minds and hearts so it illuminates every place that feels dark in our lives together. Thank You that we can have great peace because we love Your law and nothing causes us to stumble (see Psalm 119:165). Bring Your Word alive to us every day as we go through even the most difficult time in our lives. Lift our hearts up to be with Yours and clearly guide us as to what we are to learn from what we go through. Shine the light of Your Word on us like a lighthouse that leads us home to You.

I ask You to help us to always be able to communicate with each other. Keep us from the habit that many couples fall into of not talking to each other. We don't have much if we can't even talk, and that is a sign that we have lost hope in each other. Cause us to push beyond any impasse and refuse to allow the enemy of our oneness and communication to ever raise his ugly head. Help us remember that love means we *communicate* with the *one* we *love*. Help us to refuse to ever stop talking and caring about one another.

In Jesus' name I pray.

Personal Prayer Needs

_____

_____

TRUTH TO AGREE ON

Come and let us walk in the light of the Lord.

Isaiah 2:5

…that the Lord your God may show us
the way in which we should walk
and the thing we should do.

Jeremiah 42:3

In the day when I cried out, You answered me,
and made me bold with strength in my soul.

Psalm 138:3

Direct my steps by Your word,
and let no iniquity have dominion over me.

Psalm 119:133

We do not lose heart. Even though our outward man
is perishing, yet the inward man is being renewed day by day.
For our light affliction, which is but for a moment,
is working for us a far more exceeding and eternal weight of
glory, while we do not look at the things which are seen,
but at the things which are not seen.
For the things which are seen are temporary,
but the things which are not seen are eternal.

2 Corinthians 4:16-18

CHAPTER 25

Saying No to Hurtful Anger

If you ever notice anger rising up in either of you that aims to hurt the other, it's time for a reevaluation of what is exactly going on in the angry person. It has to be possible to have a serious conversation without trying to hurt each other. Hurtful anger aimed at one of you is a sign of trouble ahead because it shuts off communication. Soul-damaging anger is the kind that is constantly churning inside the angry person, who is waiting to unleash it at any given moment. And it's usually out of proportion to the offense. If rage is triggered by a simple non-offense, and the angry person seems to have no idea of what the anger is doing to the person who is attacked by it, that rage forces that person (or persons if children are also included) to walk on eggshells in order to not set off the angry person. Everyone in the family becomes afraid that anger is going to erupt again.

God has a lot to say about the foolishness of venting anger on family members. He is not pleased with it. The Bible says, "A wrathful man stirs up strife, but he who is slow to anger allays contention" (Proverbs 15:18). Someone who allays contention is a peacemaker, one who puts to rest any kind of heated argument.

Jesus said, "Blessed are the peacemakers, for they shall be called sons of God" (Matthew 5:9). If God calls you His son or daughter because you don't try to control your family with anger, what does He call you if you do stir up strife and contention with your anger? That would be a "peace-wrecker," who will not be blessed. That seems to me too high a price to pay.

If you and your spouse don't have a problem with anger, then give thanks to God that you already live by the Spirit and not your flesh. The Bible says, "He who troubles his own house will inherit the wind" (Proverbs 11:29). Anything we do that upsets our family in hurtful ways because of our anger has a price to pay for it. When you "inherit the wind," whatever you do will blow through your fingers like sand in a storm, and you won't be able to hold on to it. The Bible says, "Put off all these: anger, wrath, malice, blasphemy, filthy language out of your mouth" (Colossians 3:8).

The reason I am emphasizing this so much is because it is one of the most important concerns women listed regarding their marriage when I took a survey of women before I wrote *The Power of a Praying Husband*. And it wasn't just men who were angry. Even some women voiced concerns about their own anger in their marriage. The important thing we must remember is that we can make a *decision* to not live by anger—in our family especially. If anger becomes abusive, couples need to seek counseling as soon as possible because that is never God's will for your life. Take care of it immediately. Ask God to help you. He will.

The Bible instructs us to not let the sun go down on our anger. We are supposed to deal with it right then, before we carry it to bed with us and let it churn inside of us all night. Anger that hurts and upsets is never God's way. If that ever happens to you, agree to pray about it right then so damaging anger doesn't have control, but the peace of God does instead. Ask God to free you both from the damaging effects of this kind of anger. Don't let the enemy of your marriage and your lives win this battle. If the angry person hurts the other person with their wrath, there needs to be repentance right away, and forgiveness needs to be asked for and extended. Do it immediately. Don't give the enemy more time to do damage. Pray together that this anger will be squelched.

Anger that is hurtful damages the whole family and should never be tolerated. Let the God of peace control your life, and pray that you never have to deal with that again.

His Prayer

Lord, I praise You that Your ways never allow my wife or me to vent anger at one another in a way that is abusive or destructive. We ask that You will teach us how to love one another the way You love us so that fleshly anger never feels acceptable to us. Help us to never give way to it. Enable us to be "swift to hear, slow to speak, slow to wrath; for the wrath of man does not produce the righteousness of God" (James 1:19-20). Help us to always be led by Your Spirit and not our flesh. If I have vented my anger to my wife or other family members, show me and I will confess it to You as sin. I will also ask the forgiveness of my wife or affected family members for any hurt or upset I have caused them. Enable me to never move in the flesh but always in the Spirit. Help my wife and children to forgive me for anything I have done like that. If there have been any angry outbursts between us, help us to confess them to You and to one another. Teach us to forgive completely and agree to not let that be a part of our life anymore. We know that this type of anger only tears down what we have built together. We don't want to "inherit the wind" (see Proverbs 11:29). We want to wait on You, Lord, and inherit the good things You have for us on the earth (see Psalm 37:9).

In Jesus' name I pray.

Personal Prayer Needs

_____

_____

Her Prayer

Lord, we thank You that Your Word says that if we confess our sins, You are faithful and just to forgive us our sins "and to cleanse us from all unrighteousness" (1 John 1:9). Thank You for Your forgiveness when we come to You with repentance for any sin we have committed. Help us to be quick to confess so the enemy of our souls cannot capture us for his purpose. Your Word also says that if we have fervent love for one another, love will cover a multitude of sins (see 1 Peter 4:8). How gracious You are to us. Thank You that if we fail to live the way You want us to, we can confidently come to You with a repentant heart and confess what we have done and ask Your forgiveness, and You will grant it.

If either of us have ever exhibited destructive anger, I pray You will deliver us from the negative effects of that. Keep us far away from any anger in the future. Help us to steer clear of any trap of the flesh.

You have said in Your Word that anger "rests in the bosom of fools" (Ecclesiastes 7:9) and "a fool vents all his feelings" (Proverbs 29:11). Save us from becoming fools in hurtful ways. If we find anger coming between us, help us to confess it immediately, repent of it, and forgive each other. We know that the wrath of man will never produce the righteousness of God (see James 1:20). And that is never acceptable.

In Jesus' name I pray.

Personal Prayer Needs

_____

_____

TRUTH TO AGREE ON

Let every man be swift to hear, slow to speak, slow to wrath;
for the wrath of man does not produce the righteousness of God.

JAMES 1:19-20

Do not hasten in your spirit to be angry,
for anger rests in the bosom of fools.

ECCLESIASTES 7:9

Cease from anger, and forsake wrath;
do not fret—it only causes harm.
For evildoers shall be cut off;
but those who wait on the LORD,
they shall inherit the earth.

PSALM 37:8-9

A fool vents all his feelings,
but a wise man holds them back.

PROVERBS 29:11

Make no friendship with an angry man,
and with a furious man do not go,
lest you learn his ways and set a snare for your soul.

PROVERBS 22:24-25

CHAPTER 26

Developing the Fear of the Lord

There is great power in the two of you praying together, because when you are praying to the God of the universe in Jesus' name, it is the combination that brings the presence and power of God. But from *God's* perspective, you two not only have to agree with each other, but you also have to agree with Him. In other words, it's actually the three of you who are a threefold cord that cannot be broken. You can agree together—just the two of you—all you want, but if you aren't agreeing with God, your prayers won't have the power you need.

It's also true that *everyone needs to change* because we always need to become more like the Lord. And when you are married, that is the perfect opportunity for change because the changes that are needed are more obvious. And another thing that is obvious is that we can't make another person change. Only God can change someone, but not until that person agrees to be a willing vessel in the hands of a loving God. We who are married must have a heart that is quick to see when we could be wrong. And once we see that, we must be quick to say to the Lord, "I see where I was wrong, and I am sorry about being that way. I repent of any errors I have made." When you see your marriage and life from God's perspective, you must have a heart that is quick to repent and will allow God to change it. Pray, "Change me, Lord, to be more like You."

Another important way to accomplish the same thing is to fear God. "What does the LORD your God require of you, but to *fear* the Lord your God, to *walk* in all His ways and to *love* Him, to *serve* the LORD your God with all your *heart* and with all your *soul*" (Deuteronomy 10:12).

The fear of the Lord means having such deep love and reverence for Him that Your greatest fear is what life would be without Him. You will do whatever it takes to make sure that you show your deep love and reverence for Him every day. Having the fear of the Lord gives you a repentant heart because you want to always be willing to repent of anything of attitude, word, or action that does not please God. You would be afraid to disobey God, knowing what the consequences could be.

The promises of God to those who fear Him are many. The Bible says, "Oh fear the LORD, you His saints! There is no want to those who fear Him" (Psalm 34:9). It also says, "Teach me Your way, O LORD; I will walk in Your truth; unite my heart to fear Your name. I will praise You, O Lord my God, with all my heart, and I will glorify Your name forevermore" (Psalm 86:11-12). Of people who fear the Lord, the Bible says, "Who is the man that fears the LORD? Him shall He teach in the way He chooses. *He* himself shall *dwell* in *prosperity*, and his descendants shall *inherit* the *earth*" (Psalm 25:12-13).

When we have the fear of the Lord, we have *God's mercy*, a fountain of *life*, *protection* from *evil* to turn us away from the *snares* of *death*, the pleasure of the Lord, God's goodness, prosperity, and the blessing of inheriting the earth. All these blessings are just some of what it means to have the fear of God that are mentioned in this chapter, including the Scriptures listed in the "Truth to Agree On" section at the end of the chapter. Considering all of these, you can see how important it is for you and your husband or wife to agree about this.

His Prayer

Lord, thank You that You are the head of our hearts and minds. We choose this day to serve You above all. Thank You for how much You love us, and we give all our love to You forever. Change our hearts and minds whenever they need alteration. Make us more like You. Help us to always see what life would be without You so we never squander Your favor and grace to us by taking Your goodness lightly.

Thank You for Your Word that says, "The fear of the LORD leads to life, and he who has it will abide in satisfaction; he will not be visited with evil" (Proverbs 19:23). We are grateful for that promise, and we ask You to help us always have a deep reverence of You.

Teach us to have the "fear of the Lord" permanently engraved upon our hearts and minds in a depth that would forever keep us from losing it. Help us to always keep before us all the great things You have done for us so that we will both serve You with all our hearts and keep Your truth written in our hearts and memory. Enable us to always have such a deep love for You that nothing will ever tempt us to stray away. Keep us always open with one another, so that we don't move into a life where we live as if we are separate. If we ever lose the fear for You in our hearts and instead choose our own way, deliver us from that evil influence.

In Jesus' name I pray.

Personal Prayer Needs

_____

_____

Her Prayer

Lord, I pray that You would unite our hearts to fear Your name, as You have said in Your Word (see Psalm 86:11). Thank You for Your Word that promises if we cry out for discernment and understanding and search for both as we would a hidden treasure, then we will understand the "fear of the LORD" and "find the knowledge of God" (see Proverbs 2:3-5). Oh Lord, we seek after all that.

Help us to never be weak about what the "fear of the LORD" means in our hearts and how our reverence and regard for You encompasses and engulfs our bodies, minds, and souls. We are totally Yours—all into You—sold out completely to You and Your ways because You paid the ultimate price for us, and we are indebted to You forever. Your Word says You take pleasure in those who *fear* You, in those who *hope* in Your mercy (see Psalm 147:11). Thank You for that, because we do. Let us always be fearful of what life without You would be like. It's too horrible to even imagine, so we want to avoid those kinds of thoughts even for a moment. Let our unity of hearts regarding our "fear of the LORD" toward You never waver.

May we always have repentant hearts so we can quickly repent of anything that may harden our hearts and displease You. Help us to never try to live independently of one another or attempt to live secret lives from You or each other.

In Jesus' name I pray.

Personal Prayer Needs

_____

_____

TRUTH TO AGREE ON

The fear of the LORD is a fountain of life,
to turn one away from the snares of death.

PROVERBS 14:27

The mercy of the LORD is from everlasting to everlasting
On those who fear Him,
and His righteousness to children's children.

PSALM 103:17

By humility and the fear of the LORD
are riches and honor and life.

PROVERBS 22:4

The LORD takes pleasure in those who fear Him,
in those who hope in His mercy.

PSALM 147:11

Oh, how great is Your goodness,
which You have laid up for those who fear You.

PSALM 31:19

CHAPTER 27

Making Wise Decisions

When you are married, you have to make countless important decisions together. There are the big ticket items you must agree on, and it's good to ask for wisdom about those things. They are too expensive to make any mistakes. But there will also be times when you will have to make quick decisions that are just as crucial, and you will need the same perfect, godly wisdom. Bad or weak decisions are not an option, so it's best to pray frequently in advance so that the two of you are always covered. You will continually need godly wisdom in order to *know* and *stay in* the *will* of God. God *wants* you to know His perfect will because your greatest peace will always be there.

Jesus Himself prayed to know God's perfect will for His own life. Whenever you and your spouse pray to know the will of God, always praise God *first* because that is one thing you know is always His perfect will for you.

We can't make ourselves do God's will by just wishing on a star for it, or studying hard for it, or hoping it will work out that way. We have all seen people who are book smart but not at all wise. We don't want to take a chance on ourselves—or someone else we know—being the main source of wisdom in our life and not the Lord. You need wisdom that comes only from God, who also gives you the mind of Christ. It's possible to always have that.

The Bible says, "The fear of the LORD is the beginning of knowledge, but fools despise wisdom and instruction" (Proverbs 1:7). We don't want to ever be fools. The Bible also says that we can understand what the will of God is by being wise (see Ephesians 5:17). There is a connection between being wise and understanding the will of God. If you and your spouse frequently ask God to give you wisdom, you will have it. And when you have godly wisdom every day, you will have times when you will just know what the right thing is to do. When you have to make a quick decision, and you say, "Which way, Lord," you will know instantly what to do. You will need that ability more times than you may imagine.

Whenever you have an important decision to make, ask God for wisdom and revelation. Then praise God for His wisdom and His will and that He will reveal them to you. You will find that if you stay close to God and praise Him for the wisdom He gives you, you will more often than not know just what to do. But don't try to do this on your own. You will need to be in unity with your spouse and with God. Keep prayed up on this so you can handle those quick decisions when you absolutely need to know the mind of God.

The Bible says, "The way of a fool is right in his own eyes, but he who heeds counsel is wise" (Proverbs 12:15). It's good to pray with others about having wisdom, but start with your spouse first. Then if God reveals that you need to confer with a specific counselor for special insight and knowledge, do so. Because the Bible also says, "Without counsel, plans go awry, but in the multitude of counselors they are established" (Proverbs 15:22). There is safety in more than one godly counselor. This doesn't mean you distrust your spouse's ability to hear from God or to pray effectively. It's that the more crucial the need for wisdom regarding a specific issue, the more beneficial it is to have several counselors. But after you have heard from them, you and your spouse still need to hear from God and be in agreement about your decision.

The Bible says, "Wisdom is the principal thing; therefore get wisdom. And in all your getting, get understanding" (Proverbs 4:7). Wisdom is what you aim for, but in the process you will also get understanding. Who doesn't need that?

His Prayer

Praise You, Lord, that You are our all-knowing, all-wise God, and we thank You for imparting to us Your perfect wisdom and knowledge when we seek You for that. One of the most wonderful things about You is that You can be known. Thank You that You always share Yourself with those who love You and want to know You. You share Your love, peace, power, and will with those who worship You.

We know that just earthly knowledge alone without knowledge of You and Your wisdom will never be enough to have the blessed life You have for us. We know Your will for us is always to give thanks and praise to You. Whenever we seek to know Your will, help us to start with doing Your will in worship. Help us not trust in our hearts because that would be foolish. You are the only One who gives perfect wisdom. You give knowledge and understanding that can always be trusted. Fearing You is the beginning of wisdom for us, and knowledge of Your Holy Spirit is true understanding. Help us to always walk wisely, for that means we will be *delivered* from instead of *captured* by our own foolishness. Thank You that Your Word says Your wisdom is full of mercy and good fruits (see James 3:17). It never leaves us wondering if it is true and right. We can trust in it the way we trust wholly in You.

In Jesus' name I pray.

Personal Prayer Needs

_____

_____

Her Prayer

Lord, we thank You that You always know the way we should go. Help us to never just go off thinking *we* know the way by *ourselves* without relying on *Your wisdom*. Thank You that when we ask, You will give us wisdom, understanding, and the knowledge of Your will. We ask that You will continually guide our steps and lead us on the path You have for us every day. Thank You for Your great wisdom that You pour out on us when we seek You for it. Help each of us to make wise choices, especially with the influences we allow into our lives. We want to live Your way and follow Your leading every day.

The only way we can understand our purpose in You is if You reveal it to us. Otherwise, we might just end up guessing and waste so much time on things that will not produce all You are wanting to bless in our lives. One of the ways Your wisdom is described in the Bible is that it is pure—not diluted by doubt and questions and wondering if this is right. It also brings peace to us. It does not give us fear. We know we have a sense of hearing from You, and we feel peaceful and good about it. Enable us to always have that sense of peace and purity about Your wisdom and never a sense of doubt or feeling troubled about it. Thank You for that gentle assurance (see James 3:17).

In Jesus' name I pray.

Personal Prayer Needs

TRUTH TO AGREE ON

The fear of the LORD is the beginning of wisdom,
and the knowledge of the Holy One is understanding.

PROVERBS 9:10

He who trusts in his own heart is a fool,
but whoever walks wisely will be delivered.

PROVERBS 28:26

The LORD gives wisdom;
from His mouth come knowledge and understanding;

PROVERBS 2:6

If any of you lacks wisdom, let him ask of God,
who gives to all liberally and without reproach,
and it will be given to him.

JAMES 1:5

Happy is the man who finds wisdom,
and the man who gains understanding.

PROVERBS 3:13

CHAPTER 28

Navigating Negative Thoughts

When I was a child, I always felt depressed and anxious. I thought that was just the way I was. When I was old enough to finally figure out that no one else I knew was frightened, lonely, depressed, anxious, and about every other negative emotion I could have had, I began to figure it out. I was raised by a severely mentally ill mother who locked me in a closet whenever my father was not around and she wanted to get rid of me. We lived on a cattle ranch and later a farm with cows, horses, pigs, chickens, and fields of crops. In the off season my dad worked in the lumber mills, where he spent days at a time chopping down trees and forming them into lumber. It was hard work always, and terribly cold weather added to the difficulty and caused disaster after disaster.

One winter, a terrible blizzard killed our cattle, and that spring severe hailstorms killed our crops, and we were wiped out. So we packed up what little we had and drove west to California, where there were no terrible weather storms, and we settled there. My mother stopped locking me in a closet because I was now nine, and we lived in a house a few steps behind the gas station where my dad worked. But she was still verbally abusive, and I felt I would never escape from her miserable life.

I got away from home as soon as I graduated high school, and I started working to put myself through college. It was hard, but I eventually left UCLA at the start of my senior year to work the jobs I was actually training for and was being offered. As I shared in the introduction to this book, it was one of my coworkers in the recording and TV industry I was working in—she was a believer— who told me about the Lord and how the depressed and anxious life I was living was not what God had for me. When her pastor told me that God had a purpose for my life that was beyond what I could imagine, that is when my life changed. I learned these verses from Scripture, "Be *anxious* for *nothing*, but in everything by *prayer* and *supplication*, with *thanksgiving*, let your requests be made known to God; and the peace of God, which surpasses all understanding, will guard your hearts and minds through Christ Jesus" (Philippians 4:6-7). I lived with those verses in my heart every day.

This revelation was a monumental experience for me because it meant I had a way out of anxiety, depression, sadness, and fear, and I wouldn't have to die to get free of it all. I just had to live for Jesus and *His* way and pray about everything. I eventually found the healing and freedom I sought. I saw Christian counselors who were knowledgeable about God's ways and all He has for us. I prayed with other faith-filled believers who paved the way for many miracles in my life. This didn't all happen all at once, but something happened every time we prayed. I eventually learned not to accept less than what God had for me.

My husband, on the other hand, had found the Lord years before we were married, but he did not find the freedom from depression and anxiety that I did. His story was more traumatic and lasted a lot longer. I wrote about his situation in several of my other books. And his long journey is worth reading about. I am only telling you about what I experienced in this book because I want you to know that no matter what negative emotion you have experienced or are experiencing now, *you can get free of it.* You don't have to be miserable forever. You don't have to give up on your life. You don't have to kill yourself. God has a way out for you. He has miracles ahead for you. Don't put up with accepting negative emotions as a way of life. They are too miserable in a marriage, no matter which one of you has them.

Whether you take medicine to help you is up to you and God and your doctor. The Bible says, "Hope does not disappoint, because the love of God has been poured out in our hearts by the Holy Spirit who was given to us" (Romans 5:5). God's love for you is healing. His love and His power can break all oppression in your life and give you hope.

Because God's Holy Spirit is in you, depression, anxiety, and sadness don't own you. *Jesus does.* The enemy's plan is to steal your joy. Don't let that happen. Pray instead.

His Prayer

Lord, we thank You for Your Word that tells us we don't have to be anxious or depressed about ourselves or our lives (see Philippians 4:6-7). Whenever that happens to me or to my wife, help us to resist any kind of negative emotion that sits upon either of us and grips our lives negatively. Anoint us with Your oil of gladness (see Psalm 45:7). Help us to keep our eyes on You and take refuge in You knowing You will never leave us destitute (see Psalm 141:8). Thank You for Your promise to bring us both out "with joy" and Your "chosen ones with gladness" (Psalm 105:43).

I lift my wife and myself up to You and ask that You would free either of us when we struggle with any kind of depression, anxiety, fear of rejection, or loneliness. Your Word says You were sent to "heal the brokenhearted," "proclaim liberty to the captives," and give us "beauty for ashes," "the oil of joy for mourning," and the "garment of praise for a spirit of heaviness" (see Isaiah 61:1-3). We thank You for all that.

Help us to always walk in the Spirit so we never fulfill the lust of the flesh (see Galatians 5:17). Deliver us from every work of evil that seeks to keep us from all You have for us (see 2 Timothy 4:18). Keep us free from the torment of fear because Your perfect love in us casts it out (see 1 John 4:18). Help us to stay in Your presence where emotional liberty is found.

In Jesus' name I pray.

Personal Prayer Needs

_____

_____

Her Prayer

Thank You, Lord, that we do not ever have to be tortured with any kind of negative emotions. Search us, God, and know our hearts; try us and know our anxieties (see Psalm 139:23). Keep us both from habits that tie us to negative emotions. Let no negative emotion find a permanent place to live in either our minds or hearts. Take away any sadness or hurt. Thank You for giving us a "garment of praise for the spirit of heaviness" (Isaiah 61:3). We receive that gladly. Rebuild any place in my husband or me that has been damaged in our past. Let Your light in us evaporate any dark clouds over us.

Keep us from all negative emotions except what come immediately as a result of the trials of life, but help us to not see them as a place to live forever. Help us to keep in mind that You have the love and power to set us free. I pray that even though we may go through times that are difficult, we will not be crushed or be in despair (see 2 Corinthians 4:8). Instead of dwelling on those negative thoughts that bring us down, enable us to dwell on things that are true, noble, just, pure, lovely, good, virtuous, or are worthy of praise—the things Your Word tells us to meditate on (see Philippians 4:8), so we can be lifted up out of the dark negative-thoughts trap and into the light of the Lord. Keep us in perfect peace because our minds are focused entirely on *You*, and we totally trust in You. Thank You that You are the Spirit, and "where the Spirit of the Lord is, there is liberty" (2 Corinthians 3:17).

In Jesus' name I pray.

Personal Prayer Needs

TRUTH TO AGREE ON

Whatever things are true, whatever things are noble,
whatever things are just, whatever things are pure,
whatever things are lovely, whatever things are of good report,
if there is any virtue and if there is anything praiseworthy—
meditate on these things.

PHILIPPIANS 4:8

The Lord will deliver me from every evil work
and preserve me for His heavenly kingdom.

2 TIMOTHY 4:18

You will keep him in perfect peace,
Whose mind is stayed on You,
Because he trusts in You.

ISAIAH 26:3

The Lord is the Spirit;
and where the Spirit of the Lord is, there is liberty.

2 CORINTHIANS 3:17

God has not given us a spirit of fear,
but of power and of love and of a sound mind.

2 TIMOTHY 1:7

CHAPTER 29

Finishing Well

Finishing well" doesn't mean you cannot finish your life with a *sickness*. The title of the chapter could also be called "Finishing Strong," but you could still feel weak at the finish line. What "finishing well" means is that your character stays faithful and strong to your Lord God and to your family to the end. You don't waver in the love of the Lord and love of your spouse and children. That doesn't mean if your spouse goes to be with the Lord before you do that you can't remarry. But in doing so you don't forsake your first children for your new ones if there are any.

It means doing the Lord's will and being obedient to Him until you go to be with Him as you pass from this earth. Too often people do not stay strong with the Lord and with their family, and they let things fall apart. There are too many loose ends, and they don't take care of business. For example, plan for the time when you will be with the Lord forever. Have a will and make sure your spouse and children know who gets what. Ask them what they each want in terms of what you have. Don't let your family feel left out because nothing was ever specified. So many families split apart because things were not distributed fairly, and someone feels favored and someone else feels totally left out and hurt. Write letters of love and prayers for their future. Praying now about your future, so that you and your spouse and your children will stay tight with the Lord and each other, is worth the effort it takes to do so. Write out prayers and blessings upon your spouse and each of your children. They will mean so much.

Because of the Lord, you always have hope. You will never be hopeless. It can often feel as though your situation *is* hopeless, but because God is the Lord of hope, you are never without hope. He is "the same yesterday, today, and forever" (Hebrews 13:8). He never changes. You may go through hard times, but you will not be crushed. You can confidently place your hope in the Lord because He is unfailing.

No matter how old you are, you can commit your life to the Lord at any time and ask Him to make you both into all He created you to be. Ask Him to break down any hopelessness you feel about anything in your life, because He wants to free you from that.

The older you are, the harder it becomes to not feel insecure about the future. It's because you can grow weaker and sicker, and you begin to doubt if you can do what you used to do. And the answer is it's okay to not be able to do what you used to. That doesn't mean you are failing or not finishing well. You can instead begin to pray more, intercede more for others—even people you don't know whom God brings to your mind. Worship God more because that is always His will for your life and always pleases Him.

Even when you are waiting for something specific to happen, keep praying for others and praising God for all He is to you and all He has done for you. I knew an amazing Christian woman who was a prayer warrior her entire life. And when it became clear as she was in her eighties that she might not survive the year, she would sit up every day in her special chair and then special bed and prayed for anyone who needed prayer. People contacted her from all over the world. And she prayed until the day she died. I don't know how she felt well enough to do that, but it had to be that the joy of the Lord was her strength. No one has ever questioned whether she finished well or not. She did.

Ask God to show You the things you want to take care of while you are on this earth. Doing that doesn't mean you are going to die any minute. Not at all. Ask Him to keep you from doing anything terrible or betraying anyone. Or failing anyone. Where there is something that needs to be repaired between you and someone else, take care of it right away. There is no time like the present for repairing a mistake as much as someone will allow you to do so. Some people won't let you make amends. If that is the case, just be happy that you were willing to do so and release them to do what they want to do. You did what you could. You finished well.

His Prayer

Lord, we thank You that You call us to cast all our cares on You because You care for us (see I Peter 5:7). Thank You that the future You have for us is good (see Jeremiah 29:11). Thank You that You promise to never leave us nor forsake us (see Hebrews 13:5). Help us to have strong faith in every part of Your Word. If at any time my wife or I start to feel hopeless or weak in our faith, we ask that You will turn us around and increase our faith. Cause us to commit once again to being totally dependent on You. "Search me, O God, and know my heart; try me, and know my anxieties; and see if there is any wicked way in me, and lead me in the way everlasting" (Psalm 139:23-24). We commit to being strong and putting our hope in you (see Psalm 31:24). Give us patience to always wait for You to work in our lives.

We know that the same mighty power with which You raised Jesus, You will also raise us (see Ephesians 1:19-20). Your power will never fail, and so when it is time to meet You, You will raise us up as well. We don't have to fear You will forget us or not deem us worthy. Jesus took care of that already. We put our trust in Jesus and His love that we have received because He has made us worthy to be in heaven with You. Because You see His righteousness in us, we are eternally grateful to spend forever with You.

In Jesus' name I pray.

Personal Prayer Needs

_____

_____

Her Prayer

Lord, I thank You that Your plans for us are always good and never evil, and You have promised us a good future and a great hope (see Jeremiah 29:11). Thank You that You are always able to do more than we can ever imagine according to Your power at work in us (see Ephesians 3:19-20). We continue to put our hope in You. We commit our lives to You again and ask You to take away any hopelessness from our thoughts because You are our God of hope. We wait on You to renew our strength so we can run and not be weary (see Isaiah 40:29-31). Thank You that You always hear our prayers no matter what we go through and no matter how long we wait for Your answer. We will not give up because You who have begun a good work in us will finish it until we go to be with You (see Philippians 1:6). Therefore, we will not give up and listen to the enemy's lies. We will only listen to Your truth and trust in that. Help both of us to be ready to be with You whenever that time comes when You call us home. Help us to finish our race with joy (see Acts 20:24). Thank You that when we cry out to You, You will always hear us and deliver us from all our troubles (see Psalm 34:17).

Help us to plan for the time when we leave this earth by writing letters to each of our loved ones with what we pray for them to receive from us in terms of a spiritual inheritance and anything we want them to have that we know they would want. Guide us clearly in all we need to do to not leave any loose ends for our loved ones to sort out.

In Jesus' name I pray.

Personal Prayer Needs

_____

_____

TRUTH TO AGREE ON

Since we are surrounded by so great a cloud of witnesses,
let us lay aside every weight, and the sin
which so easily ensnares us, and let us run
with endurance the race that is set before us.

HEBREWS 12:1

I have fought the good fight, I have finished the race,
I have kept the faith.

2 TIMOTHY 4:7

I have glorified You on the earth.
I have finished the work which You have given Me to do.

JOHN 17:4

I know the thoughts that I think toward you, says the LORD,
thoughts of peace and not of evil, to give you a future and a hope.

JEREMIAH 29:11

It is not in man who walks to direct his own steps.

JEREMIAH 10:23

CHAPTER 30

Keeping Your Eyes on the Prize

You go through many different things when you are married, and often you get through each situation that arises without too much of a challenge. You can pray through them, and talk through them, and God helps you to rise above them. But sometimes you come up against a situation that feels as if it could be a game changer if something doesn't change. You think it may never change at all, so you can grow tired of the problem and have no patience for it any longer. You can become weary and worn down. You wonder how much longer you can do this if nothing ever changes. But the truth is, you *can* get beyond whatever it is that causes these problems if you both see that this could be the complete breakdown of your marriage if God doesn't do a miracle in both of you.

It helps if the two of you *keep* your *eyes* on the *prize waiting* for *you* at the *end* of your *life*. But when it comes to praying for change, sometimes you don't have to wait that long. God wants to save, restore, and preserve your marriage now, and He wants to bring both of you closer to Himself and to each other. Even when you can't see how anything will ever change, God can. And He *can do miracles*.

The Bible says, "Weeping may endure for a night, but joy comes in the morning" (Psalm 30:5). You may wonder, *What morning will that joy be coming?* You know you can't make a miracle happen by yourself. It takes three: you, your spouse, and God. You have to put your hope entirely on God and say as Jesus said, "With God, all things are possible" (Matthew 19:26). And that is a promise to anyone who believes God and loves Him with all their heart.

These are the times when you have to keep your eyes fully on the prize. There will be a time when you meet the Lord at the end of your life, and you want to be able to say, "There is laid up for me the *crown* of *righteousness,* which the Lord, the righteous Judge, will give to me on that Day" (2 Timothy 4:8). We can't forget what a great day that will be.

You also want to hear at the end of your life, when you stand before God, the words of the Lord to you, saying, "Well done, good and faithful servant; you have been faithful over a few things, I will make you ruler over many things. Enter into the joy of your Lord" (Matthew 25:23). I know that can seem like a faraway impossibility, but you can't lose hope in that. God can always do a miracle, and He will. We just don't know when because we live on His timetable. Paul said, "I have learned in whatever state I am, to be content" (Philippians 4:11). That is something great we all need to ask God for.

I have written in a couple of my books that as long as you continue to walk with the Lord and never turn your back on Him, then you are always going from *glory* to *glory* and *strength* to *strength* (see 2 Corinthians 3:17-18). It may not seem like it at the time, but it's true when you walk faithfully with Him. "In the way of righteousness is life, and in its pathway there is no death" (Proverbs 12:28).

The truth is, "if anyone is in Christ, he is a new creation; old things have passed away; behold, all things have become new" (2 Corinthians 5:17). That holds true for your entire life. So, "let this mind be in you which was also in Christ Jesus" (Philippians 2:5).

Always remember that God's resurrection power is what raised Jesus from the dead. And that same power will raise you who believe in Him now and forever. All of these things are part of the prize God has for you both.

God gives us a crown if we live according to the rules. That is, we don't make up our own rules and try to live that way. We need to run the race with our eye on obtaining the prize. Athletes do it for a prize that perishes. We do it for a crown that *never perishes* (see 1 Corinthians 9:24-25).

Whenever you feel you can't go another step the way things are, pray this to God, "Turn away my eyes from looking at worthless things, and revive me in Your way" (Psalm 119:37). Don't give up. Stay the course. Run the race to receive the prize. Jesus endured the cross "for the joy that was set before Him" (Hebrews 12:2). Pray you can do the same with His help. At the end of your life, the prize is to be with the Lord forever and wear the crown of life He has promised to give you. What greater joy can you have?

His Prayer

Lord, we worship You, our God of glory, and thank You that You have for us a future that is greater than anything we can ever imagine. You are "not the author of confusion but of peace" (1 Corinthians 14:33). Thank You that You have given us the mind of Christ (see 1 Corinthians 2:16). Thank You that You give us clarity and allow us to see things from Your perspective. I ask this day that if either of us ever feels as if we are stuck, or defeated, or hopeless in any way, that You would lift our eyes to the hills where our help comes from. It comes from You, who made all of heaven and earth and beyond (see Psalm 121:1-2). Thank You that You never slumber nor sleep, and You will watch over us always and keep us safe, even when we are sleeping (see Psalm 121:4). Thank You that You preserve our souls so that we will be with You forever (see Psalm 121:8).

Help us to never lose heart or feel so hopeless that we want it all to end because You are always our hope, and we can look to You every day for every need we have. Help us to never give up on You because You will never give up on us. We will always look forward to the joy that is set before us by being in Your presence forever.

In Jesus' name I pray.

Personal Prayer Needs

_____

_____

Her Prayer

Dear Lord, thank You for sending Jesus. Thank You, Jesus, that You gave Yourself on the cross for us. Thank You, God, that You not only raised Jesus up from the dead to live with You forever at Your right hand, but You have promised to raise us up also when we pass from this earth by Your same power. Help us to never lose sight of the fact that our greatest prize is being with You forever in heaven (see 1 Corinthians 6:14).

Whenever we feel sad or discouraged by what has happened in our lives, we ask that You would lift our eyes up to You, where we can always see Your goodness, mercy, and grace. Thank You for turning our mourning into dancing. Let us not clothe ourselves in sadness, but allow You to clothe us with Your joy and gladness. We sing Your praises and will not be silent because we want to give thanks to You forever (see Psalm 30:11-12). Help us to keep our eyes on the prize, which is living in Your presence for eternity. Help us to set aside every weight, disappointment, and snare the enemy sets before us. Mold us together with You and each other so that we can run this race before us. Help us to forget all that is behind us so we don't live with regret, because You want us to look forward to the eternal beauty of the holy place that is prepared for us in heaven with You.

In Jesus' name I pray.

Personal Prayer Needs

_____

_____

TRUTH TO AGREE ON

Blessed is the man who endures temptation;
for when he has been approved, he will receive the crown of life
which the Lord has promised to those who love Him.

JAMES 1:12

If anyone competes in athletics,
he is not crowned unless he competes
according to the rules.

2 TIMOTHY 2:5

Do you not know that those who run in a race all run,
but one receives the prize?
Run in such a way that you may obtain it.

1 CORINTHIANS 9:24

I press on, that I may lay hold of that
for which Christ Jesus has also laid hold of me...
forgetting those things which are behind and
reaching forward to those things which are ahead,
I press toward the goal for the prize
of the upward call of God in Christ Jesus.

PHILIPPIANS 3:12-14

Looking unto Jesus, the author and finisher of our faith,
who for the joy that was set before Him endured the cross.

HEBREWS 12:2